GETTING TO KNOW GOD'S WORD

HOW 66 BOOKS OF THE BIBLE TELL GOD'S REDEMPTION STORY

DENNIS C STEVENSON JR

CONTENTS

LET'S DIG INTO THE BIBLE

How could a collection of ancient manuscripts tell a story that makes sense today?

How could a writing process spread over fifteen hundred years and at least thirty-nine authors tell a story that connects?

It defies logic that the Bible could be any more than a fragmented and disjointed mess of out-of-date exhortations and irrelevant stories.

The exact opposite is true.

Through many authors and long timeframes, the Bible tells a tightly choreographed story of God's redemptive love. Despite the diversity of foreign cultures and strange landmarks, the Bible speaks urgently to us today about our spiritual condition and need for a Savior.

Many people pick up their Bible and start reading, only to be confused and overwhelmed by all the strange details. But if we take a step back to see the larger pattern and organization of the stories in the Bible, the entire book makes sense. The key to understanding the Bible lies in seeing how the books fill in the details of a much larger message. Once we focus on that greater structure, each of the individual pieces falls into place.

A Brief Overview of the Entire Bible

After God created the world and made Adam and Eve the on-site managers, Adam made a selfish decision. By choosing what he wanted and disobeying God's command, Adam altered the course of human history and passed his rebellion on to all of his descendants.

This introduced the fundamental question of the Bible: How could the effects of Adam's decision be reversed?

Many years later, God chose a family to be His special people. They were an inauspicious group who grew into a great nation. He bound Himself to them and revealed His standard to them. Yet, time after time, they rejected God's loving relationship and willfully turned away from Him.

God repeatedly appointed leaders to deliver the people from the consequences of their selfish choices. But once the immediate crisis was over, they turned back to their wicked ways and soon found themselves in trouble again. When they asked for a king to be a human intermediary between themselves and God, He graciously granted their request. Sadly, most of the kings were wicked men who led the people farther away from God.

God appointed special spokesmen who reminded the people of God's goodness and the price of disobeying Him.

Rather than heeding the words of these divinely inspired messengers, the people disregarded them and mistreated them. God's words fell on deaf ears, and the people ignored God to pursue their agenda.

Despite the rebellion of God's people, the Bible documented what a proper, godly life looked like through the lives of an obedient few. Through poetry and wise advice, anyone seeking holiness could understand how to live. But most people ignored righteous living in favor of selfish interests.

So, God punished the people at the hands of foreign oppressors. Ripped from their homeland, He sent them far away to live under the rule of enemy empires. But God did not abandon them, and after a time, brought them back to their homes again and re-established the temple where they could worship Him.

Then God stepped back and waited for the time to be right.

If we've learned anything up to this point, it's that no human effort or institution could offer a solution to the problem of redeeming humanity. Every opportunity to serve God had failed. The result was a spiritual disaster.

How could God make things right? After thousands of years of every human effort, how could a permanent solution happen?

At just the right time, God sent His Son to be born as a human. He lived a life that fully satisfied God's righteous standards. Instead of enjoying the benefits of His relationship with God, He gave His life and exchanged His righteousness for the penalty of sin. As a result, those who believe in Him can enjoy a redeemed relationship with God–just as if they had lived up to God's standards.

After God's Son returned to Heaven, His work on earth continued through the power of the Holy Spirit, who came just as He promised. He established the church, and the message of redemption spread over the whole earth. People from every nationality and culture joined this church through faith in the sacrifice of Jesus.

In the first years after the church began, error crept in. God appointed men who had known Jesus to offer encouragement, correction, and instruction on how to live properly in this new relationship with God. These men wrote letters that the church has saved and remain as the authoritative instruction on how we should live redeemed lives.

But God is not through. He has shown how he will bring an end to this current situation. Jesus will return, this time not to suffer, but to reign. He will judge the earth and will deliver the consequences of Adam's rebellion to all who stand before God without a Savior. He will recall the wickedness that went unpunished in this life, and each person will receive the full measure of God's wrath.

But for the redeemed, God's wrath will not come. He has already poured it out on Jesus. Instead of wrath, they will enjoy a new creation centered on God. And they will worship God forever.

In summary, this is the story that we find in the Bible. It is one of loss leading to hopelessness, of love leading to sacrifice, and death overcome by life. Every chapter of every book of the Bible contributes to this marvelous story.

God is the Author of the Bible

While we don't have a single narrator describing the events as we read, the Bible tells us that God, through the Holy Spirit, superintended the writing of scripture. The Holy Spirit was the mastermind behind the organization and message of the Bible. God didn't leave it up to individual people to communicate His message. He orchestrated the entire thing. From start to finish, His fingerprint is on every page.

Because God was intimately involved in writing the Bible, we know that the Bible accurately reveals Him and His plan. Through it, we discover who He is, what He is like, and what He has done. In the pages of scripture, we learn what He loves and what He hates. When we talk about God, we are talking about what we've learned about Him through the Bible, validated by our own experiences.

Of course, individual authors brought their style to it. We see Solomon's wise words in Proverbs. Paul's impeccable logic drives his epistles. Samuel's storytelling makes 1 and 2 Samuel flow like a novel. James's practicality moves naturally through his letter.

The Holy Spirit wasn't a dictator in His inspiration. We see a celebration of diversity in the styles of writing throughout the Bible. But despite the differences, the message was directly from God. It was His way of revealing Himself to us.

Traditionally, the Bible follows a roughly chronological pattern. That's why most Bibles have Genesis first and Revelation last. Genesis begins with "in the beginning" and Revelation ends with eternity future.

But there is more than that. This organization of the Bible also follows a thematic organization. It's convenient that this also mostly aligns with the chronological view.

- Genesis through Deuteronomy are the Books of Moses or "The Law"
- Joshua through Esther are History books.
- Job through Song of Solomon are Wisdom books
- Isaiah through Malachi are "The Prophets"
- Matthew through John are the Gospels
- Acts is a New Testament History book
- Romans through 3 John are Epistles or letters
- Revelation is a New Testament prophetic book

The chronology moves forward through time. However, History and The Prophets overlap and address concurrent events. They are the same chronology told from different perspectives. Some authors of the Wisdom literature were also contemporaries of the History books.

From Moses (who wrote the first five books) through Malachi (the last Old Testament writer) was about a thousand years. Throughout that time, holy writing was coming out regularly. The Old Testament features thirty-nine individual books and some of the longest ones at that. The Holy Spirit didn't exactly have an editorial calendar, but except for the four-hundred-year period that the book of Judges describes, there was a cadence of communication from God.

Then came the great silent period. After six hundred years of nearly continuous communication, even if much of it was condemnation, God seemed to go silent. Between Malachi and Matthew, everything seemed to stop. This was unnerving for the people of Jesus' time. It was like God had forgotten about them.

Then, after Jesus' ascension into Heaven, there was a burst of activity. Twenty-seven books came out in approximately forty years. And then they stopped again. It's been almost two thousand years since the ink dried on John's Revelation of Jesus Christ.

We now consider the revelation closed. That doesn't mean that God is done. Just that His communication is complete. He's told us everything we need to know. We certainly have enough to understand the gospel and follow lives of spiritual growth.

For this book, we'll start with Genesis and end with the Revelation of Jesus Christ. Between these two bookends, I've divided the narrative up into eleven different segments.

1. In The Beginning: Genesis 1-3
2. God Chooses His People: Genesis 4-50
3. God Chooses Leaders: Exodus–Judges
4. Give Us A King!: 1 Samuel - Esther
5. The Wisdom in the Middle: Job–Song of Solomon
6. God's Spokesmen: Isaiah–Malachi
7. The Life and Times of Jesus the Christ: Matthew–John
8. The Birth of the Church: Acts
9. The Spread of the Church: Acts
10. Error and Instruction: Romans–Jude
11. And Then Comes the End: Revelation

When we look at the Bible through this framework, the unifying thread of God's story becomes clear. Not only that, but we will also see how the structure of the Bible ultimately and finally tells the story of salvation.

INTRODUCTION TO THE OLD TESTAMENT

PART 1

We call the first section of our Bible the Old Testament. It contains 39 individual books that span the time frame from the creation of the world to the return of the Jewish exiles from Babylon. It is called the "Old" Testament because the books it contains are the oldest writings of the Bible.

A major theme of the Old Testament is God's relationship with the nation of Israel. In Genesis, we read how God selected one family out of all the people on earth and promised to dedicate Himself to them to be their God. With few exceptions, the Old Testament describes this ongoing relationship between God and His people.

A major feature of the Old Testament is the institution of the sacrificial system which Moses started on behalf of God. It began with the Tabernacle, a traveling tent-temple in which God made His resting place on earth. Later, with King Solomon, the place of worship shifted to a permanent temple. Only at the altar and with a proper sacrifice could the faithful gain a covering over their sins before God.

Much of the Old Testament centers on the Law. This is the body of instruction that God gave to Moses. The Ten Commandments are a famous element of The Law, but it contained many more instructions beyond those ten. It described God's holy standard of living. It pointed out sin and proscribed the means of dealing with that sin.

Throughout the Old Testament, the people of Israel struggled with the Law. They often disregarded God's instructions and flirted with the pagan worship practices of the surrounding people. Despite their unfaithfulness, God remembered His promises to them. While He frequently punished their disobedience, He always restored them to favor when they repented.

The entire Old Testament was written before Jesus was born. The Jewish religious leaders collected and assembled this group of ancient books and identified them as the Word of God. As Jesus grew up, the Old Testament was His scripture. Throughout His ministry, He quoted from many of the books we find in the Old Testament.

1

IN THE BEGINNING

GENESIS 1-3

If we want to follow the story of the Bible, we should become familiar with the characters we'll be reading about. The first 3 chapters of Genesis introduce us to the protagonists, antagonists and the fundamental conflict that will continue throughout the whole Bible.

Each of the chapters introduces one new character in a developing drama. By the end of these three chapters, they will have made a terrible mess of everything. We'll be left wondering what God could do to restore the situation.

The Protagonist

The protagonist is the person who the story is about. We think of them as the "good guy" that we want to cheer for.

Genesis 1 identifies the protagonist by the fourth word:

> In the beginning, God...

It's easy to say that God is the good guy. He's the author of the story, but He's also one of the main characters.

The entire first chapter of Genesis is all about God in action. Through the revelation to Moses, who wrote the book of Genesis, we meet God and understand what He's like.

The first thing we see is God's power. Genesis 1:1 summarizes that idea when it says, "In the beginning, God created the heavens and the earth." This simple sentence points us back to God as the creator of everything.

The process of creation is something we are familiar with. We talk about creating a painting, or a kitchen table, a blanket, or even a tasty meal. We call this activity "creation" because it seems like at one point the thing didn't exist, then it did!

In reality, whatever we created existed before we got involved. It was just in a more basic form. The paint was still in the tube; the table was a stack of lumber; the blanket was just a fold of fabric; and the meal was uncooked and unseasoned. What we call creation is more like transformation.

God had a different take on creation. When God started His creation, nothing existed. He didn't transform the matter from one form to another. He created matter, then shaped it into what He wanted. Scholars call this *ex-nihilo creation*: Creation from nothing.

When we read Genesis 1, if we are paying attention, we will recognize right away that God's kind of creation is way beyond anything we have ever seen or done. The amount of power it would take to call matter into existence and then give it a specific form is spectacular.

Another thing we see about God is His satisfaction with what He created. By the end of Genesis 1, we see God has moved through six periods of creation. At the end of each one, God reviewed it and passed judgment: "It is good."

We all have varying standards of what makes up "good". Some of us have high standards, others have relatively low standards. But God's standard is unwavering. To be good, something must be completely good. It can't have any aspect that isn't good.

When God called His creation good, He meant it was exactly what He had intended to create. No part of it fell short of His creative plan. He didn't have to guess in a few spots and hope it would work. He envisioned all of creation, and what He made perfectly aligned to that vision.

Our Point of View

The end of chapter one introduces us to the second main character: man and woman. We know them today as Adam and Eve. In this part of the story, they were the only human beings in existence. As time passed, they would have children and humanity would grow to the billions that we find on Earth today.

Adam and Eve were just like us. Or, perhaps more accurately, we are just like them. As we read the story of the Bible, we will see it through their eyes and from the perspective of their descendants. From this point onward, humanity will play a central role in the development of the biblical narrative. We will observe all of God's actions through the perspective of the people who were there to experience them.

God was very particular about creating human beings. He held a council with Himself and declared two intentions:

1. To make human beings in His image
2. To give them dominion over the things that He had created.

The first decision was interesting because it implies that everything else that God had created up to this point did not bear His image. This set the man and the woman apart from the rest of creation. They were not like other created things (fish, birds, animals, light, dark, sun, moon, stars, water, etc.). God invested some aspects of Himself in people that He held back from the rest of His creative work.

The second decision helps us understand what it meant to be created in God's image. God said that the function of human beings would be to have dominion, or rule, over the other things He had created.

In Genesis 2, we read a more detailed account of how God created Adam and put him in the Garden of Eden with instructions to take care of it. Adam was like God's on-site manager for all of creation. God gave Adam the right and the duty to tend the garden on His behalf. It's hard to imagine what kinds of gardening God needed Adam to perform for Him. But the Bible is clear that caring for the garden was Adam's responsibility.

Part of Adam's dominion over the garden was the right to eat of its bounty. Beyond just being the caretaker, Adam could use the garden for his benefit. He needed to eat, and God told him that the entire garden was available to him.

Of course, this freedom came with some boundaries. One specific tree was off-limits. God told Adam this tree would kill anyone who ate of it. The Tree of the Knowledge of Good and Evil was not for food.

With the instructions complete, God gave Adam his first task: go name all the animals. Adam went around and started giving names to everything he saw. Aardvark, Alligator, Armadillo... Just as God exercised His authority by naming what He had created in Genesis 1, Adam exercised dominion over the animals by giving them names.

After looking at all the animals and how they had companions, Adam understood he was alone. In response, God provided Eve as his perfect compliment. It overjoyed Adam to see another person. God blessed them both and commanded them to be fruitful and populate the world He had given them to administer.

The Antagonist

So far, we have a pretty cheerful story. God created a glorious world and put Adam and Eve in it to take care of it for Him. If you thought that sounded too good to be true, you'd be right.

In Genesis 3, we meet the third major character: The Serpent.

While we would think of a serpent as a snake, it's clear that this snake was not anything like snakes we know today. So, we'll assume that this serpent was much more than just a snake. Later, we'll give him different names, like Lucifer or Satan. But in Genesis, he was just called "the serpent".

Based on what the serpent said, it's clear that he was not a part of God's wonderful creation. In his first recorded conversation, we find him trying to undermine God's authority and subvert the management structure that God put in place. It's easy to see that he had positioned himself as the enemy of God.

What's amazing is that God knew the serpent was there yet chose not to destroy him. For a God who could create the entire universe out of nothing, getting rid of a troublesome snake wouldn't be difficult. But God opted not to take such extreme measures.

The serpent plays a brief but pivotal role in Genesis 3. In one short conversation, he set events in motion that would ruin the perfect harmony of the world God had just created. It was what he wanted to do because he wanted to establish his own control over creation.

The serpent met Eve in the garden and commented about how tasty the fruit on the Tree of Knowledge of Good and Evil looked. Eve agreed with him, but remarked that God had told them to leave the tree alone. The serpent countered with an accusation that God wanted to keep her in the dark because if she ate from the tree, she would be just like God. This appealed to Eve because she wanted a taste of that knowledge, so she picked the fruit and took a bite.

Adam was there because Eve simply handed him the forbidden fruit. Adam knew she had broken God's rule and would suffer the consequences. But he was so in love with her he followed her lead and ate the fruit as well. This meant he would not live forever and watch her suffer alone and die. He would join her in whatever punishment God would bring.

At this moment, the serpent got exactly what he wanted. He created a rift between God and the people He had created. When God came walking in the evening to chat with them, they hid because they were afraid of Him. In one action, Adam and eve ruined Paradise.

The Conflict

Every story needs a conflict. Now we have a conflict of biblical proportions.

God entrusted Adam and Eve to care for the wonderful garden He had created. He only gave them one rule. And they broke it. By rebelling against God's rule, they also rejected God and shifted their loyalty to the architect of the sinful path they had taken.

Adam no longer worked for God to care for the garden. He had decided another way was better and turned his back on God. He stood under God's judgment and condemnation and would eventually die. The serpent and his wicked ways were now pulling Adam's strings.

This is the fundamental conflict that runs throughout the rest of the Bible. Through Adam's sin, every person who has been born partakes in that same rebellious attitude. God didn't just lose Adam's loyalty; he lost the allegiance of everyone who followed Adam. Slaves to sin and condemned to death, every person ever born is guilty of violating God's holy standard and must receive the wages of that sin.

Everything points back to that one decision in the garden. Before eating the fruit, Adam and Eve enjoyed evening time chats and walks through the garden with God. But one bite shattered that relationship, and neither Adam nor Eve could put the pieces back together again.

We might think that God could just call "do-over!" He could say, "I won't count that one." If He was God, He could remake the rules.

Except God had to remain true to His character. To violate who He is would be just as bad as Adam and Eve sinning. Because He had to uphold His holy nature, He could not embrace sin. Since He had already made the pronouncement, "In the day you eat of it, you will surely die." He was bound to that course of action.

So, what would happen next? How would God restore His creation? How would He get His image bearer back?

The Promise

It didn't take long for God to intervene. He called Adam, Eve, and the serpent together to pass judgment on their actions. While they were there, He had something to say to each of them about how things would change.

God cursed the serpent and promised that a descendant of the woman would oppose him. While the serpent would cause pain and agony for the descendant of Eve, this opponent would crush him and defeat him.

Eve had to look forward to painful childbirth, and her relationship with her husband would involve conflict.

Because of Adam's sin, God cursed the ground. This changed Adam's harmonious relationship with the earth to require toil and sweat to produce what he needed. And when he died, his body would decompose and return to the earth.

While the situation seemed ruined, hope was on the horizon. Adam and Eve were going to die at war with God. The serpent had effectively hijacked God's splendid creation. But God had not given up and had a plan to address everything which had just gone off the rails.

Genesis 3:15 is a beacon of hope in this dark situation.

> *"I will put enmity between you and the woman,*
> *and between your offspring and her offspring;*
> *he shall bruise your head,*
> *and you shall bruise his heel."*

Sin and death, the result of the serpent's deception, would reign over all of humanity. But the serpent and a descendent of Eve would battle each other. The result would be difficult for both, but the descendant of Eve would get the upper hand and be victorious.

This verse contains God's promise to send a redeemer who would create a way for us to come back to Him. He also declared that He would bring about redemption through a descendant of Adam and Eve. Even though sin separated them from God, He would not abandon them completely.

Adam and Eve received short-term bad news. Life was going to get rough. The glorious existence they had known was going to change. They were going to die. But in the long term, God had a plan to address the spiritual consequences of their actions.

The rest of the Bible tells the story of how this plan played out as God took steps to redeem what had been His.

Gospel Application

The gospel is the climax of the Bible. It's the pivot point upon which everything hinges. As we read God's word, we need to keep the gospel in mind.

Even though the story of creation is far removed from the life of Jesus in the gospels, it sets the stage for the good news. We discover the need for good news because this story is all about the bad news.

If this was the end of the story, it would be dark and depressing. Cut off from God and without hope, we could never experience what God had intended in the Garden of Eden. Contaminated by sin and marked by death, our only destiny would be judgment.

Genesis chapter three gives us a glimmer of hope and a glimpse of the gospel plan. God committed to change the order of affairs and redeem what He created. But at this distance, it's far off and not very clear.

The first few chapters of Genesis set the stage for the rest of the Bible. We witness the first disobedience and observe the great chasm between God and the people He created. Now we need to see how God will fix this seemingly insurmountable obstacle called sin.

God's actions relative to sin and redemption are a reliable roadmap to follow as we look at all the rest of the sections of the Bible. So, each chapter will end with a review of how the gospel appears in the ongoing saga of redemption.

2

GOD CHOOSES HIS PEOPLE

GENESIS 4-50

We're only three chapters into the Bible, and already a lot has happened. We don't know how long Adam and Eve enjoyed the garden before the events of Genesis chapter 2 ruined everything. But when it all went sideways, it didn't take long.

God played the "Good Guy" of the story. He created everything out of nothing. Such was His creative power that everything He made was good. It was not missing anything. In every respect, it aligned exactly to what He intended.

We met the "Bad Guy" in the serpent. He wanted to be on top, and when he couldn't have that, he spoiled the one thing God created "in His own image." So, the serpent attacked Eve with crafty words and convinced her it was in her best interest to eat from the tree of which God had said, "in the day you eat of it, you will die."

Finally, we see Adam as the guy in the middle. Once he saw Eve eat the forbidden fruit, he knew he had a choice. Despite being created in God's image, despite being placed in the middle of a perfect garden, despite chats with God in the evenings, he made a selfish decision and went with Eve, even if it meant the grave.

Even though we didn't get the chance to experience the beauty of the garden or enjoy chats with God, we share in Adam's consequences. This shouldn't come as a surprise since we confirm his decision every time we individually sin and fall short of God's standard.

God kicked everyone out of the Garden of Eden and posted an angel with a flaming sword at the gate to ensure that nobody came back and ate of the Tree of Life. Humanity was moving in one direction, and it was the opposite direction from what God intended.

This leaves us with a question: "How is all of this going to be made right?" It's frustrating to see how good it could have been, but one decision destroyed everything. Was there any hope for humanity? Would God ever get His original plan back on track?

With these questions in mind, we move into the rest of the book of Genesis. It's a long book, fifty chapters. It tells the story of seven people:

1. Adam–which we've already read.
2. Abel (and Cain)
3. Noah
4. Abram (later renamed Abraham)
5. Isaac (Abraham's son)
6. Jacob (Isaac's son)
7. Joseph (Jacob's son)

The next 6 people show us how God moved. Having lost Adam, and through him all his descendants, God chose a people He would call His own. It was the beginning step in a redemptive process that stretches across the entire Bible.

Cain & Abel

After the expulsion from the garden, we read of Eve giving birth to two brothers. Cain was the older, and Abel the younger. As they grew, these two boys chose unique paths. The Bible describes Cain as a "worker of the ground" and Abel as a "keeper of sheep." Cain was a farmer, and Abel was a shepherd.

When the time came to bring an offering to the Lord, each young man brought the fruit of his hands. Cain brought the most succulent produce he had grown. Think of the reddest tomatoes and the biggest cucumbers you've ever seen. Abel brought a lamb or two and sacrificed them.

God accepted Abel's offering and rejected Cain's. We aren't told how God communicated His acceptance. It could have been something dramatic, like fire consuming one and leaving the other. Or perhaps it was a communication in a dream. Either way, both men knew God had accepted Abel's offering and not Cain's.

Later in the Bible, we gain some additional insight into the two sacrifices. Hebrews 9:22 says, "without the shedding of blood there is no forgiveness of sins." It's possible that Abel's offering met the requirement because his sacrifice was the only one that shed blood.

Hebrews 11:4 looks back at this story and proclaims that Abel gave his offering in faith. Perhaps Cain did not. Cain may have been just going through the motions, and because of that, God rejected his gift.

The end of this story was as tragic as that of Adam and Eve. Consumed by anger and jealousy, Cain killed his brother. Unwilling to be excluded, he destroyed the one whom God had blessed.

In this brief story, we see that not everyone would follow God. From the very beginning, some people gained God's approval and others did not. But how would God choose the people through whom He could work? Since nobody was perfect and sin tainted everyone, the choice wasn't obvious.

Noah Found Favor

We next encounter Noah's story. Most people know this story. God told Noah it was going to rain when it had never rained before. His instructions to Noah were to build a big wooden ark in which to save his family and the animals of the world from drowning.

Before Noah pounded the first nail, however, we need to look at the run-up to the story. God looked down from heaven upon the situation on the Earth and came to a sad conclusion:

> The LORD saw that the wickedness of man was great on the earth and that every intention of the thoughts of his heart was only evil continually. And the LORD regretted that he had made man on the earth, and it grieved him to his heart.
>
> (Genesis 6:7)

This is exactly the opposite of the "it is good" judgment that followed the steps of creation. After letting humans have their way for a while, God was full of regret for His creation because it no longer reflected Him or His glory.

If we stopped here, it might sound like this story was going to be short! God had decided that the situation on Earth was so bad that His only option was to destroy all living things. Maybe He would start over again.

In one of the great turnarounds of the Bible, the very next verse says, "But Noah found favor in the eyes of the Lord."

The Bible describes Noah as righteous and blameless, one who walked with God. Noah did not take part in the wickedness of his day. Rather than living for himself, he lived for God. We don't know the details of Noah's daily practice, but he understood who God was, and that God had a different standard than everyone else.

With the forecast of a major rainstorm coming, God gave Noah the plans for the ark and kicked off the century-long building project. Noah endured the curiosity, then the ridicule of his neighbors as he slowly built this enormous vessel. He and his sons labored alone to craft it according to the design God provided. And then God brought the animals, two-by-two, as we like to sing. And Noah ushered them all into the ark.

When God finally closed the door, He would not open again until His judgment was complete. Then the rain fell. It was a novel concept until the water on the ground puddled, then the puddles turned into lakes. For forty days and nights, the rain fell until the water covered the face of the earth. That deluge drowned all life.

Through the flood, we experience the judgment God desired in Genesis 6:7. God destroyed all humans, animals, and things that crept about on the earth. But God preserved Noah and his family. And to continue life on earth, God preserved one family of every living animal.

Noah's story shows us how God chose specific people to be the recipients of His favor. He worked through them to bring about the results that He wanted to accomplish. It offered a small taste of what God's plan would be like.

But the promise of Genesis 3:15 would require much more than a global flood and a small family. God was just getting started.

Abraham - Father of Nations

Using the genealogies of Genesis as a guide, Noah was still alive when Abram was born in Ur. The world was three hundred years post-flood, and Noah's lesson hadn't stuck in the mind of the people who lived then.

When he was seventy-five years old (middle age in those days), God called Abram out of his hometown in Mesopotamia to a new place. In faith, Abram picked up and moved, not sure where he would end up. His faith pleased God, and God chose Abram and his family to be a special people.

Genesis 15 describes a unique conversation between God and Abram. When God promised that Abram's reward would be great and his descendants would be many, Abram believed God. Genesis says that God counted his belief as righteousness. Even though Abram was a sinner, God saw his faith and credited that to his account.

When God continued and promised that Abram would possess the land on which he walked, Abram asked a simple question.

"How do I know this is going to happen?"

God didn't have a material sign to give Abram. There wasn't a deed waiting for him around the corner at the local title store. So, God made a promise, but through a strange ceremony. He commanded Abram to bring a young cow, a goat, a sheep, and a couple of birds. Abram killed them and cut them in two, laying the halves with an empty path between them.

The strange sacrifice which was described is the ceremony that was used when two kings made a treaty. The person walking the path between the animal halves was saying, "may I be like these animals, split in half, if I break the promise I am making." It was the strongest kind of language and a contract that God would keep His promise.

Genesis 15 describes that God alone walked between the animal halves. This means that God bound Himself to Abram and to his descendants. Abram could not break the treaty because he never swore to perform anything. All the commitment was upon God.

The treaty God made with Abram had four components:

1. Abram's family would be vast and numerous–although Abram and his wife Sara were childless.

2. God would give Abram a land to call his own–although many Canaanite tribes occupied the land.
3. God bound Himself to Abram and the family that would come from him.
4. Through Abram's family, God would bless all families.

Before this four-fold covenant, God had chosen individual people who lived righteously and walked by faith in Him. Genesis mentions Abel, Enoch, and Noah as three such people. This covenant changed all of that. Rather than God choosing those who lived properly, He had bound himself to one family line.

This means God would be bound to His people, but they could reject Him and live any way they wanted. As we study further, we'll see that's exactly what happened. But for now, we see God was picking one family tree and connecting Himself only to that family to accomplish His goals, as promised in Genesis 3.

When Abraham had died, and his son Isaac was carrying on the family line, God appeared to him as well. In Genesis 26, God re-affirmed His commitment to Isaac.

> I will be with you and will bless you, for to you and your offspring, I will give all these lands, and I will establish the oath that I swore to Abraham, your father.
>
> (Genesis 26:3)

In ratifying the covenant with Isaac, God clarified He was choosing the line of Isaac to affirm His promise. God excluded Abraham's older son, Ishmael, and the children he had by his second wife.

Isaac had two sons. He named the oldest Esau and the youngest Jacob. As these boys grew, they chose different paths. Esau was the hunter, and Jacob was the gardener. God chose Jacob, the younger brother, to receive the blessing he had offered to Abraham and Isaac. In Jacob's famous vision of the stairway to heaven, God reiterated yet again the same promise that He had made to Abraham and Isaac.

1. Jacob's descendants would be many

2. They would have a land to call their own

3. God would be with them

4. Through these great people, God's blessing would extend to all peoples.

Once again, God excluded one son from the promise. It flowed down through Abram, Isaac, and Jacob. By the end of Genesis, we read Jacob had twelve sons. These sons each because of the leader of a clan or tribe of their descendants. From them, we get the twelve tribes of Israel.

Over three generations, God narrowed down and focused His attention on a single family. He bound Himself to them and promised them great numbers and a land to call their own. Through this one family, He would work to accomplish all His promises in Genesis three.

The Proof is in the Pudding

In the last act of the book of Genesis, we see proof of God's active care and protection of this family. Ten of Jacob's sons became jealous of one of their brothers. In an act of incredible cruelty, they sold him into slavery and lied to their father, saying a wild animal had killed him.

What they didn't know was that God had a plan for Joseph. While they meant to punish the brother they loathed, God used this rejected son to provide a path of salvation for the entire family. Joseph knew God and knew how to follow Him. While in Egypt, he did not abandon his faith. Because of this, God warned him of a great famine coming and he told Pharaoh to stockpile grain against the lean days to come.

While the brothers sold Joseph as a slave, God arranged for him to become the Grand Vizier of Egypt. He became second in power only to the Pharaoh. Through God's provision, while the region suffered in hunger, Egypt had grain to spare. When Jacob's family ran out of grain in Canaan, God used the bounty of Egypt to save them.

God was holding up His end of the bargain. He had taken the children of Abraham, Isaac, and Jacob to be His people and set them up with the provisions they needed. Against all odds, they prospered when all others struggled.

This brings us to the end of the book of Genesis. It ends on a favorable note. God had chosen His people. He had saved them from famine and set them up in a beneficial situation in Egypt. They were not yet as many as the stars of the sky. They did not yet have a place to call their own. But they were enjoying God's favor.

Gospel Application

This section of the Bible shows the terrible effects of sin. Affairs on earth became so bad that God regretted He had created the world. If Genesis three was dark, what followed became pitch-black.

But God showed His grace through the life of Noah, and then through Abraham, Isaac, and Jacob. He did not allow the situation to become hopeless. He preserved a family line committed to serve Him.

Each of these men showed faith. They believed God would do what He promised. And based on their faith, God would deliver them from death and judgment.

Hebrews 11 talks about the Heroes of Faith and lists these men in the "Hall of Fame". Their faith allowed God to work through them and bring about the plan of salvation instead of destruction and judgment.

Toward the end of Genesis, through the life of Joseph, we get a foreshadowing of what God planned to do. Unjustly sold into slavery and with his life on a trajectory that was pointed toward tragedy, God used Joseph as the agent of salvation for his family. It was an unlikely outcome given the start. But God showed how He could use His lowly servants to achieve great things.

Through this part of the Bible, God chose the tools He would use to architect our salvation. He started by picking one family and working through them to achieve His purposes. The promises He made to them reinforced the promise in Genesis 3 that blessings and a Savior would come.

3

GOD CHOOSES LEADERS

EXODUS - JUDGES

For three generations, God had made a promise to one family in the ancient Middle East. It was an unbreakable covenant that they would become a great nation and live in the land that God would give them. God would grant His favor to them, and through them, He would bless all nations.

At the end of the book of Genesis, God miraculously provided for His people by sending Joseph to Egypt to prepare for the famine, then sending the rest of his family to live in comfort there.

Only one problem remained.

God's people were stuck in Egypt, far from the land God had promised them. Pharaoh, the king of Egypt, didn't want to let them go, and Canaanite kingdoms ruled in the promised land.

To be true to His promise, God had to lead His people out of captivity in Egypt, into the Promised Land, and give them victory over their enemies. Situations like this called for strong leadership. So, God raised leaders for His people. Without them, the Israelites would have remained in Egypt and God's plan would have stalled out.

From the book of Exodus through the book of Joshua, we read the story of God's plan in action. The children of Israel didn't make it easy, and there were some long detours on the path that God laid out for them. But God was faithful to appoint leaders in Moses and Joshua who did not waver and followed Him faithfully.

Time and time again, God's people got into trouble. When they finally cried out to God, He responded by appointing a new leader to lead them out of their problems. But when the crisis was past, the leader retired, or eventually died, the people returned to their willful way and another round of trouble would come again.

Out of Captivity

After Joseph died and his memory faded, a new Pharaoh came to the throne who didn't owe him a debt of gratitude for saving the nation. Likewise, this Pharaoh didn't think it was a good idea to give preferential treatment to the Hebrews. By this time, they had become so many that Pharaoh feared an uprising. So, he made them into slaves who worked on his grand building projects.

Moses entered the story. Even though he was born to Hebrew parents, Pharaoh's daughter adopted him into her household. Growing up, he received an education suitable for a prince of Egypt. He lived a privileged life that contrasted with the plight of his countrymen.

But as a young adult, Moses had some serious character flaws. Exodus 2:11-12 briefly tells how he murdered an Egyptian who was beating a Hebrew slave. The Bible doesn't spend many words on the story, but it paints a picture of a man with a hot temper, who thought he was above the law.

This one action ruined Moses' life of luxury. We might have thought that he was on the path to do great things to aid his people. Instead, he fled Egypt before news of his crime brought down the wrath of Pharaoh.

The next time we meet Moses, he had been herding sheep for forty years. This was what he needed to prepare him for the task God had for him. Drawn to a burning bush, he had a face-to-face encounter with God and received his leadership assignment: Lead My people out of Egypt.

Moses would have known how impossible that task was. He knew how many people there were. Pharaoh would never allow it to happen. They would face obstacles trying to get out of Egypt. Eventually, the army would get involved, and they didn't have a military force that could defeat the Egyptians.

Fortunately, God wasn't counting on anything Moses could do to defeat Pharaoh. God had a plan to bring Israel out of Egypt. But He needed a leader to make it happen. The leader was someone the people could see and listen to and follow. The leader modeled the faith in God that the people were to imitate. God would speak to the leader, then the leader relayed the message to the people.

Moses went to Pharaoh, just as God instructed, and told him to let the Hebrews go. Pharaoh refused, so God rained down ten plagues on Pharaoh and Egypt. The plagues discredited

Egyptian gods, ruined the Egyptian agricultural economy, and killed the firstborn of every household in Egypt. When Pharaoh finally had enough and demanded that the Hebrews leave, God caused the people of Egypt to give them gold, silver, gems, and garments. On their way out, the people of Israel plundered the Egyptians without raising a weapon.

But Pharaoh eventually reconsidered and wanted his slaves back. So, he sent his chariot army after the rag-tag band of Hebrews wandering in the desert. The army pinned Moses and the Israelites against the Red Sea, and the situation looked hopeless.

But God had them exactly where He wanted them. He caused a wind to blow all night and open a dry path through the Red Sea. The Israelites walked through the waters and reached freedom on the other side. When the Egyptian army tried to follow, God released the waters and drowned the heavily armored army. Without a single soldier, God defeated the Egyptian army in a humiliating fashion.

The influence of leadership and the closeness of his relationship with God had a profound impact on Moses. In Numbers 12:3, we read "Now the man Moses was very meek, more than all people who were on the face of the earth."

This was quite a far cry from the murderous young prince. It shows that God was bigger than the problem and bigger than the leader himself.

Moses' mistakes didn't throw God off course or turn His plans ruined. God's primary requirement for a leader wasn't political connections, or a can-do attitude, or even persuasive eloquence. God had all those things and more to spare. He was looking for a man who would love and serve him.

Moses led the Children of Israel for forty years. He received the Law directly from God on Mt. Sinai and communicated God's standards and expectations for His people. He wrote the first five books of the Bible as God's spokesman.

God was on the move. He was leading His people out of Egypt. He used Moses, the flawed leader, to put the plan in motion. But this wasn't the end. More leadership was required.

Into the Promised Land

Who wants to follow a hero? Conventional wisdom says that following a beloved leader is a hard task. That was exactly what Joshua faced. He had been Moses' lieutenant for almost 40 years in the wilderness. He had waited patiently while God punished his generation for their lack of faith. But now God had chosen him to be the leader of these stubborn and rebellious people.

God called Joshua and gave him a pep talk.

> "Have I not commanded you? Be strong and courageous. Do not be frightened, and do not be dismayed, for the LORD your God is with you wherever you go."
>
> (Joshua 1:9)

God wanted Joshua's attention. This was not Joshua's chance to try out all the ideas that he'd read in management and leadership books. God wanted Joshua to be courageous because he was operating under God's wisdom and power. This wasn't about Joshua. This was all about God, and God wanted to make sure Joshua understood.

God gave Joshua the plan. To Joshua, it must have been crazy. It was full of impossible tasks that he could never accomplish on his own. But God reminded him again to be courageous and have faith.

Following the chat with God, Joshua didn't waste any time. He immediately issued marching orders and got the people moving. God had given him the plan, and he put it into effect right away.

Step one of God's plan was to cross the Jordan River. Normally, this was not a hard task. The Jordan River did not rank among the great rivers of the world. But this was flood season, and the waters were raging. Crossing the raging river with a host of people was a risky move.

God's instructions were clear: walk into the river. Just do it. Joshua told the people, "The Priests with the Ark of the Covenant are going to walk into the raging river. Watch!" So, they did. And God stopped the water of the flooding river so that the nation walked across on dry land.

This terrified everyone in the land of Canaan. Crossing the flooding river was completely unexpected. It displayed God's power and reminded them that their gods had done nothing so magnificent.

Step two of God's plan was to conquer the heavily fortified city of Jericho. That was a monumental task. The king of Jericho had seen Joshua and the people coming and he was doing everything he could to defend his city.

God's instructions were equally clear: walk around the city. This was not in any military handbooks or taught at any of the military colleges of the day. Taking a fortified city meant a siege, and possibly a battering ram, and maybe trying to dig under the walls. But this wasn't what God wanted.

Joshua made the people walk around the city every day for a week. On the last day, they packed a lunch and made the circuit seven times and then blew their horns with all their breath. That's when God knocked the walls down. The people of Israel just had to climb over the rubble to take the city.

Up to this point, Joshua had been doing very well. He had followed God's instructions and had overcome two seemingly insurmountable obstacles with divine solutions. But because of that, God got the credit, and the region fell deeper into fear of the Israelites and their God.

Joshua led the Israelites to conquer the land God had promised to Abraham, Isaac, and Jacob. Under his leadership, the people subdued most of the people that lived in the region. They divided up the territory and gave each of the twelve tribes a region to live in.

The plan seemed to unfold just fine. Joshua was a good leader, and his willingness to follow God brought about the promised outcome. Finally, the children of Israel had a place to call their own. God's promise was coming true.

Joshua was the model of a servant leader. He knew where his power came from. Joshua was humble enough to let God be big and strong. He didn't need to take power into his own hands and make the situation all about him.

Before he died, Joshua called the people together and told them the secret of his success was that he had followed God. He made them swear that they would follow God when he was gone. He was confident that God would bless them if they continued to follow Him.

Victory over Their Enemies

It seems Joshua set up the people of Israel for a happily ever-after ending. God was on their side. The promise was being fulfilled. Everything was looking up.

But the Israelites were only partially obedient. Where God had told them to eliminate all the Canaanite kingdoms, they didn't finish the job. Pagan influences remained around them and they didn't seem to care.

When Joshua and his leadership team were gone, the slow slide became an avalanche. The people abandoned the God who had brought them out of Egypt and had so miraculously given them the land. The people turned away from God and they did what was evil in God's sight and worshipped the gods of the people of Canaan.

The book of Judges talks about what happened after Joshua was gone. Throughout the book, we see the same pattern repeated over and over. The people disobeyed God and worshipped Canaanite idols, so He brought in an enemy to conquer them. When life seemed to be unbearable and the people finally cried out for help, God chose a judge to free them and bring them back to Him. This lasted for a while, but then the cycle began again.

Judges 4-5 tells the story of Barak and Deborah. As predicted, the people had returned to practices that angered

God. So, God made them subject to a Canaanite king. He had a powerful chariot army and terrorized the region for twenty years. Finally, the people cried out to God for help.

God already had His person on the ground. Her name was Deborah. She was both a prophetess and a judge. The people came to her to decide matters, and she made godly judgments on their behalf. When God heard the cries of His people, He spoke to Deborah, and she called upon a man named Barak to raise an army and lead an uprising.

Barak lacked the faith to obey God. He wouldn't take the assignment unless Deborah went to war with him. He was more worried about Jabin's chariots than he was confident in God's power to defeat them.

Deborah agreed to go, but added a stipulation from God. Because Barak didn't have the faith to follow God on his own, God would deny him the glory of capturing and killing the enemy commander. God would give that privilege to a woman.

Events happened just as Deborah had said they would. Barak and his army went up against the forces of Jabin. God gave them into Barak's hand, and he routed the enemy. Sisera, the enemy commander, fled for his life. Barak pursued, but Sisera escaped.

Sisera ran as far as he could. When he was about to drop from exhaustion, he came to a tent where a woman named Jael lived. Sisera asked for water, but Jael craftily gave him warm milk and covered him with a blanket. Being exhausted, he fell asleep. When she was sure he was out, Jael took a tent peg and pounded it through Sisera's temple and into the ground.

Barak and Deborah introduced a short period where the people followed God. But when they were gone, the people reverted to their old habits. They returned to the gods of the Canaanites and resumed the worship of idols.

Once again, God became angry and brought an army from the kingdom of Midian to punish them. Every time the Israelites harvested their crops, the Midianite army would sweep in from the East and steal the grain. Finally, the people cried out to God, and he heard their pleas.

God chose a man named Gideon to be the leader and defeat the Midianites. With God on his side, Gideon proved to be an effective recruiter. Soon he had an army of thirty-two thousand men. But God didn't want a large army, so He told Gideon to dismiss 99.9% of the recruits.

God wanted to show His power. He wanted His people to remember who He was. He made sure there was no chance anyone would think military effectiveness lead to the victory that would follow.

One night, while the Midianite army slept, Gideon deployed his three-hundred-man army. They hid in the hills around the enemy camp with covered torches and trumpets. At Gideon's signal, they uncovered the torches and blew their trumpets.

When the Midianites woke to the trumpet blast, God confused them. They couldn't tell friends from foe and started fighting with one another. Those who survived turned and fled, seeking safety. Gideon and his soldiers pursued them until he had captured and killed their leaders. The rest of the army scattered.

The people of Israel looked at Gideon with hero-worship after that. They rightly saw the favor of God upon him. They asked him to become their king and establish a dynasty of rulers. Gideon declined.

Gideon said to them, "I will not rule over you, and my son will not rule over you; the LORD will rule over you." (Judges 8:23)

Gideon had the right answer when the temptation came to exalt himself over God. He understood that the victory had been all God's doing. He was just the leader that God had selected to be a part of the divine plan.

For the rest of his life, Gideon judged the people of Israel. While he was alive, they followed God. But when he died, they turned back to the idols of the Canaanites.

The Consequence of Leadership

Throughout this section of the Bible, we see how God's focus had settled on the people of Israel. He was fulfilling His promise to Abram, Isaac, and Jacob. Instead of waving a divine magic wand, He chose leaders to achieve the results.

One of the constant lessons that we see from this section of the Bible is that despite divinely appointed leadership, the people of Israel continually choose to ignore God. Whether they were grumbling in the wilderness, failing to subdue the Promised Land, or worshipping the local idols, the people repeatedly turned away from God.

Fortunately, God regularly appointed new leaders to bring the people back to Him. He didn't become frustrated or weary with this repetitive action. This was only one part of the greater plan. He still had the problem of Genesis chapter three to solve. But when the time was right, He wanted His people to be ready.

Gospel Application

Once again, the story of redemption got stuck in a dark place. But God showed His power by delivering His people out of Egypt. When the children of Israel had no power themselves, God worked through them and their circumstances to achieve the outcome He wanted.

Through these actions, God showed His faithfulness and His ability to deliver on His promises. This is important to the gospel because if God couldn't keep His promise to Abraham, Isaac, and Jacob, then it wouldn't be likely He would keep the much more challenging promise to Adam and Eve.

Through God's dramatic deliverance and provision of land for His people, we saw how He continued to lay the foundation of the plan for redemption. The plan had a lot of steps, and it was comforting to see them happen, even if the culmination of the plan wasn't entirely clear yet.

God also introduced the Law in this section of the Bible. The Law communicated His definition of holy living and the standards that He demanded. Unfortunately, the Law only pointed out violations. It did not show the path to holiness. It served as documentation of failure and reinforced the judgment that Adam and Eve brought upon all humanity.

This section of the Bible introduces the question, "If we can't please God when He is directly involved and delivers

His people and appoints leaders to show the way, how can we overcome the problem of sin?"

Even the best leader failed. Moses could not enter the Promised Land as a punishment for a single angry outburst that dishonored God. If Moses couldn't please God, how can we hope to please God?

Every time God selected a Judge, the relief was only temporary. Invariably, God's people turned their backs on Him as soon as the crisis had passed.

These observations cause us to cry out for a more permanent solution. God's plan couldn't stop at miraculous deliveries and temporary judges. We needed something that would work better than that.

4

GIVE US A KING!

1 SAMUEL - ESTHER

We now come to the next section of the Bible: 1 & 2 Samuel, 1&2 Kings, and 1 & 2 Chronicles. These historical books describe the Kingdom period of the nation of Israel. It lasted about 460 years and saw a fresh development in the civic life of Israel: transformation into a kingdom under the rule of a human king.

First Samuel introduces us to the last judge of Israel: Samuel. The first few chapters set the stage for how God selected Samuel from the service of the tabernacle. Soon, Samuel was the leading spokesman for God, a man who judged the nation and served as a focal point for all things related to governance and religion.

Give Us A King!

The trouble seemed to start when Samuel grew old and tried to pass the mantle of leadership to his sons, who were not godly men like him. The people of Israel sent their tribal leaders to Samuel with an ultimatum: Give us a king like the other nations!

Samuel knew this would not turn out well. Not only was it a repudiation of his leadership and his parenting, but it was also going to open the door for many other problems that the Israelites hadn't experienced to this point.

God knew this wasn't the actual issue. The problem was much deeper. In 1 Samuel 8:7-9 God instructed Samuel:

> "Obey the voice of the people in all that they say to you, for they have not rejected you, but they have rejected me from being king over them. According to all the deeds that they have done, from the day I brought them up out of Egypt even to this day, forsaking me and serving other gods, so they are also doing to you. Now then, obey their voice; only you shall solemnly warn them and show them the ways of the king who shall reign over them."

Samuel obeyed God. When it came time to warn the people of what would happen under a king, he didn't spare them at all. He gave the tribal leaders a laundry list of the trouble they would experience under a king.

1. He would conscript them into service for his pleasure
2. He would tax them to fund his administration and pay for all the officers he employed
3. He would take their sons and make them into soldiers for his army

4. He would take their daughters to work in his palace as servants and cooks
5. Ultimately, the people would become his slaves

This didn't bother the Israelites, and they renewed their demand for a king. God told Samuel to do what they requested, and he grudgingly followed God's command.

Saul–The First King Of Israel

Even though the people asked for a King, God was still the one to decide who it would be. When Samuel had sent them away after agreeing to their demands, God chose the man whom He would anoint as king.

Saul, son of Kish of the tribe of Benjamin, was an obscure man. His family was insignificant in the tribal structure, and the tribe of Benjamin was one of the smallest of all the tribes. But he was tall and handsome.

Saul made a dashing king. His family was wealthy, so he had enjoyed a good life as he grew up. Now he was a full head taller than all the men of Israel. His size alone made him look kingly. But his face and hair were attractive too. Essentially, he was a picture-perfect king.

God arranged for Saul to meet Samuel while out searching for some lost donkeys. Secretly, Samuel honored him and anointed Saul with oil. Samuel told Saul about a series of amazing and specific things that were going to happen on the way back home to his father's house. They happened just as Samuel had prophesied–evidence to Saul that God had chosen him to be the king over all of Israel.

Later, Samuel called all the tribes of Israel together for the official coronation. They drew lots to narrow the selection by tribe, then family, finally down to the person. The lots chose Saul, son of Kish, the tall, handsome specimen of a young man. When Saul stood before them, head and shoulders taller than anyone present, the people cried out, "Long live the king!"

Several years into his reign, Saul had behaved exactly as Samuel had foretold. He had assembled an army of three thousand men. They were in the southwest of Israel, dealing with a rising threat from the cities of the Philistines. The Philistines mustered an army over ten times the size of Saul's and rode out to meet him.

Saul knew he was in deep trouble, so he called for Samuel to come to him and intercede with God for Israel. Samuel replied he would come in seven days. Saul waited, and when the seven days had passed, worried that the Philistine army would attack soon and seeing that his army was scattering, Saul himself offered a sacrifice to God asking for a favor in the upcoming battle with the Philistines.

Just as Saul finished the offering, Samuel arrived. Samuel was furious that Saul had overstepped his bounds and disobeyed God, for only a priest could offer the sacrifice. When he confronted Saul, the king could only offer his excuse that the people were deserting and if he hadn't done something, the army would have deserted him.

> Samuel replied, "You have done foolishly. You have not kept the command of the LORD your God, with which he commanded you. For then

> the LORD would have established your kingdom over Israel forever. But now your kingdom shall not continue. The LORD has sought out a man after his own heart, and the LORD has commanded him to be prince over his people because you have not kept what the LORD commanded you."
>
> 1 Samuel 13:13,14

Just like that, Saul disobeyed God, and Samuel told him that his dynasty had ended before it even began. God was going to choose another man to be king next, a man who loved God and who would obey Him.

Throughout the life of Saul, we see how God desired obedience over everything else. Saul served as a life-sized object lesson about how God views disobedience and rebellion. Just as He dispensed justice on Adam in the Garden of Eden, God also brought justice upon Saul, even though God had originally chosen him to be the king.

King David–A Man After God's Heart

After God rejected Saul as king, he sent Samuel to anoint the next king. Samuel went to the home of Jesse of Bethlehem, in the tribe of Judah. When he arrived, he asked to meet Jesse's sons. They were all strong and handsome. They looked like excellent candidates to be the next king.

Samuel knew that God had chosen none of them. He asked if there were any others. Jesse responded that there was David, but he was out in the fields, watching the flocks.

David, who was still young and not yet considered a man, was not suitable to be introduced to the great Judge. Samuel replied he wouldn't eat until he had seen David.

When he met David, God told Samuel that this was the man who would be King. Samuel uncorked his horn of oil and anointed David in front of his older brothers and father. At that moment, the Spirit of God rushed upon David and remained with him from then on.

Saul was still king, so David went back to his sheep. His family shrugged off what they had seen and returned to life as normal. It wasn't until later when David defeated Goliath that he became famous.

After Goliath, Saul invited David into his household as one of his servants. David got a front-row seat to see how Saul operated as a king. But as God withdrew His favor from Saul and showed it to David, Saul turned on David and tried to kill him. Eventually, David was driven out of Saul's court and became a man on the run.

David remained in exile for the rest of Saul's reign as king. They played a high-stakes game of cat and mouse throughout the Judean wilderness. Saul wanted to eliminate his rival so his son could take the throne after him. David waited on God's timing to become king as Samuel had anointed him.

Within a few years of Saul's death, David became the King over all of Israel. David spent most of his forty-year reign at war with the enemies of God's people. His military success established and secured large the borders of the kingdom of Israel.

David's desire was to build a proper house for God. Ever since the exodus from Egypt, the people of Israels had worshipped God in a traveling tent. David wanted to honor God with a beautiful temple in Jerusalem.

God answered David and said he had chosen another man to build a temple. That task would fall to David's son. But God had something else for David.

> "Your house and your kingdom shall be made sure forever before me. Your throne shall be established forever."
>
> 2 Samuel 7:16

God promised He would establish David's family as a dynasty that would last forever. David would not suffer the same fate as his predecessor Saul, whom God had rejected. God saw David's heart and recognize David's dedicated to Him. Later, God would describe David as, "a man after my heart, who will do all my will." (Acts 13:22)

Once again, God unilaterally committed Himself to a family. This time one family out of all the families who descended from Abraham, Isaac, and Jacob. This family would be the royal family of His people and would have the right of rule for all time. God had chosen again and was narrowing down how He would reclaim what He had lost in the garden.

This was the king God desired. One who would obey Him and follow His commandments. God knew he would fail and sin when He promised to establish David's dynasty as an eternal line of kings. Yet God also knew David's heart and that David loved Him and would respond appropriately to His sin.

The Kingdom Divided and Conquered

When David died, rule passed to his son Solomon. Solomon enjoyed peace throughout his life, in part because of the conquests of his father. He built a temple to God, a magnificent building that proclaimed the greatness of God through its beauty.

In a dream, God appeared to Solomon and offered him anything he wanted. Rather than choosing riches or fame, Solomon asked for wisdom to rule God's people. Pleased with this answer, God gave him wisdom, but also long life, riches, and fame.

But when Solomon died, his son Rehoboam inherited the throne. At his coronation, the people who were weary of the taxes his father had levied asked him what kind of king he would be.

Rehoboam, however, lacked his father's wisdom. He listened to bad advice and finally answered the people foolishly. He promised to double-down on the taxes and make his father's burden look light. Upon hearing this, ten of the tribes, all in the north, decided they no longer wanted to be ruled by the house of David. They returned home and rejected all authority from Rehoboam in Jerusalem.

This created a new political system for the children of Israel. Ten of the tribes split off from David's dynasty and followed a new king named Jeroboam. The remaining two tribes, Judah and Benjamin, continued to be ruled by David's descendants. The two kingdoms became known as Israel in the north and Judah in the south.

The history of the northern kingdom of Israel only featured kings who rejected and disobeyed God. Over a string of nineteen successive kings, not even one honored or obeyed God. They actively led Israel astray and worshipped false gods.

Ultimately, God's punishment came. The kingdom of Assyria, the greatest military power in the region, conquered the northern ten tribes and deported them to live far away. In return, they brought in foreign subjects and settled them in the territory that had once belonged to God's people.

In the kingdom of Judah, however, twenty generations of the house of David and Solomon reigned in unbroken succession. While most of the kings were wicked like their northern neighbors, eight followed God. Because of the faithfulness of these eight kings, Judah lasted 130 years longer than the Kingdom of Israel. However, punishment eventually caught up to them when the Babylonians conquered them in 586 BC.

Lessons from the Kings

The book of Samuel focused on the lives of Saul and David. It gives us an intimate insight into the lives of the first two kings and God's perspective on how He wanted the king to rule over His people.

God was very clear to Samuel that He was the ultimate ruler of His people. However, He delegated that ruling authority to specific kings to administer in His stead. Just as with

Adam, that delegated authority went awry, demonstrating that sinful human beings would not obediently follow God regardless of the circumstances of their lives.

Kings and Chronicles offer parallel accounts of the kings of Judah and Israel. The book of Kings begins with the life of Solomon and continues the narrative begun by the books of Samuel. The book of Chronicles begins with genealogies, including the genealogies of the exiles who returned from Babylon. Likely written after the Babylonian captivity, it reminded the people of Israel of their special heritage and relationship with God.

Collectively, these six books in our Bible describe the failure of human rulers to provide the righteous leadership that would satisfy God. Even those rulers who followed God were flawed and suffered the consequences of sin. But most of the leaders, despite the miracles God had done in their past, turned their backs on God.

The overarching lesson of these six books is to point out the need for a ruler who would not lead God's people to destruction. Human leaders were incapable of the leadership needed to find a way back to God. Even though God hand-picked the people He wanted, they still failed.

As we chart the trajectory of the story told in the Bible, the crisis is becoming increasingly dire. In Genesis chapter two, sin entered the world. Yet, after all these events, humanity was no closer to a solution for the problem of sin than they were when the first sin happened.

But God's plan was developing. He had chosen His people and had been fulfilling His promises to them. He put leaders in place, but those leaders sent the people astray, directly into punishment at the hands of foreign armies.

The books of Ezra and Nehemiah offer hope. They tell how God remembered His promises. The people of the kingdom of Judah, after seventy years of captivity in Babylon, returned to their homeland. It was a hard journey, but they rebuilt the walls of Jerusalem and constructed a new Temple where they could worship God again.

They suffered punishment for their unfaithful actions, but it was not the end. God was gathering His people again to continue the story of the Bible.

Gospel Application

The books of history focus on the kings of Israel and Judah. They bring into sharp focus two primary lessons that we need to learn.

The futility of human leadership

Through almost forty kings, we see that a human king is not the answer to the problem of sin. Kings and governmental systems could not provide the relief that was desperately needed.

Even when a king served God, he eventually died. Leadership passed to the next king, who might be a king who did not fear God. This inconsistency brought about dramatic variations in the faithfulness of the people. None of the kings provided a permanent solution to the problem.

The impact of leadership

As goes the king, so go the people. When the king loved and served God, that trickled down to the people. It required strong leadership to make that happen.

But when the king acted wickedly, so did the people. Unfortunately, most of the kings fell into this category. The time of the kings was a time characterized by unfaithfulness by the people of Israel. Often led by wicked leaders, they pursued their agendas and disobeyed God.

From a gospel perspective, again, we face the need for a permanent solution that would not depend upon the heart of a human leader. Redemption would not come about through any human circumstances. It would require something greater than human to provide the ultimate solution.

God promised David an eternal throne. In this covenant, we see a glimpse of the greater plan which would provide for an external king. This king would rule forever and lead in a way that glorified God.

5

THE WISDOM IN THE MIDDLE

JOB - SONG OF SOLOMON

Until this point, our journey through the Bible has been a chronological narrative. We started in Genesis with the creation and the fall, then worked forward through time as God chose His people and led them, ultimately giving them a king.

In the last chapter, we saw the kings didn't work out very well for God's people. Despite kingly leadership, they failed to follow God, ultimately resulting in God's judgment and punishment.

The last of the historical books, Ezra and Nehemiah, finished the historical arc of ancient Israel on an upward trajectory. God remembered His people. He didn't leave them in captivity in Babylon. He brought a remnant back to their ancestral homeland around Jerusalem. They lacked their former glory, but they were home.

We're going to leave this storyline for a while and shift focus. If you follow in your Bible, the next five books take a new direction. No longer are they about history, but they introduce a new topic that we will stop to consider.

In the middle of the Bible (by page count), we find the section called "Wisdom Literature." It's a series of books that don't fit in anywhere else. They don't follow the narrative pattern that we've been enjoying until this point. They don't seem to hang together in the same way that the History books told a single story.

If you didn't have a biblical background, you might think that this was the dumping ground for all the misfit books. These books have a common theme. It's not historical or narrative. These books are all linked by a similar idea or topic:

Wisdom.

In today's culture, we usually think of wisdom as being associated with intelligence or experience. Perhaps you've heard wisdom defined as "knowledge applied". That's not a poor answer. But in this case, it's a suitable answer to a different question.

Most of us think about wisdom as defined by the original rationalists–the Greeks. Their word for wisdom, Sophos, gives us words today like "sophisticated". You can see the idea of intelligence or smarts buried at the root of this word.

When we read about wisdom in the Bible, however, we're looking at a completely different time and language. The "wisdom literature" of the Bible draws from an ancient Middle Eastern notion of wisdom.

In that culture, the wise person lived the "good life". This person offered a model of living to be emulated by others.

They had done it right and had their priorities and values in correct alignment. They focused on what mattered and ignored what was temporary or less important.

> 'Behold, the fear of the Lord, that is wisdom, and to turn away from evil is understanding.'
>
> Job 28:28

From a biblical perspective, the wise person lived a godly or God-fearing life. This didn't mean that they had snappy answers to all of life's problems and challenges. But they knew what was important and how to set their priorities. In return, they experienced the blessings of God. This didn't always appear as a material blessing. Even the wise person could suffer. But the wise person had a proper perspective when hard times came upon them.

The fundamental question considered through the wisdom section in our Bible is, "How can a person live a life that pleases God?"

There are five books in the section of our Bible that we traditionally call "The Wisdom Literature."

1. Job
2. Psalms
3. Proverbs
4. Ecclesiastes
5. Song of Solomon

Each of these books has a different perspective on wisdom and gives us unique lessons on what the "good life" looks like.

Job–A Perspective on Suffering

Job was a God-fearing man who lived in antiquity. The Bible describes him as blameless and upright. Not only did he fear God, but he actively turned away from evil. So attuned was he to the fear of God, every time his kids threw a party, he would offer sacrifices on their behalf lest they, in a fit of revelry, should say or do something unrighteous.

Satan Challenges: God Accepts

Very early in the book of Job, we read of Satan visiting God in heaven. When God remarked about His servant Job, Satan countered to say that Job only loved God because of the material favor God had poured out on him.

God permitted Satan to persecute Job, up to but not including taking his life. The wager was that when the blessings vanished, Job would stop loving God. Satan left heaven ready to unleash a world of suffering on Job that would crush his spirit and turn him against God.

The first round of suffering focused on the things Satan thought Job would hold dear. First were his children, then his vast estates and herds of livestock. In one devastating raid, Satan took them away from Job.

Job's response to this calamity was to fall to his knees and worship God. He did not accuse God of wrongdoing. He said, "If I enjoyed what God gave me, then I have no reason to complain when He takes it away."

Satan doubled down by taking Job's health. Beset by pain, Job tried to care for himself, treating boils and plague-like symptoms. Even with this turn of events, Job would not accuse God of anything wrong.

Job's wife was not so patient. Having watched as everything disappeared, she had a very different reaction. Astutely, she understood that this was a spiritual attack. Yet she did not have the right perspective on it. Her advice to Job was "Curse God and let Him kill you and be done with it."

Job rejected her advice, clung to his faith in God, and simply waited.

Such was the fall of a prominent man in the community that Job's friends soon came to commiserate with him and offer him advice. Three such friends came and sat with Job for a week, offering no judgments or advice.

Finally, when they could take it no longer, they shared their advice. In a word, it was all terrible advice. They did not show wisdom. From a human standpoint, it all sounded good. It was just wrong.

The dialog between Job and his friends began in chapter 2 and continued for most of the book. It followed a pattern where each friend made a case for Job's guilt and identified his circumstances as God's just punishment for some unknown sin.

Job answered each of his friends and challenged their advice. Throughout his answers, he consistently claimed that he was blameless before God and that God could bring whatever circumstance He wanted into Job's life.

Job did not know of God's arrangement with Satan. His friends could only look at the circumstances and apply worldly logic to figure out what was going on. Job said he didn't understand, but that he was blameless for the outcome. His friends continued to challenge him to admit his guilt and repent so that God's mercy and grace would continue.

Job Clings to His Redeemer

In the middle of this argument with his friends, Job presented his core belief that God's justice would be served.

> "Oh, that my words were written! Oh, that they were inscribed in a book! Oh that with an iron pen and lead they were engraved in the rock forever! For I know that my Redeemer lives, and at the last, he will stand upon the earth. And after my skin has been thus destroyed, yet in my flesh, I shall see God, whom I shall see for myself, and my eyes shall behold, and not another. My heart faints within me!
>
> Job 19:23-27

In this great proclamation of faith in God, Job laid out his faith, that even if he were to die from his circumstance, he would still stand before his Redeemer. Job understood that this was all about God and not at all about him. God's holiness and justice would prevail, and Job's present condition would not cause any shadow upon God's character.

Finally, in chapter 38, God entered the discussion and spoke to Job. God asked Job, "Can you do my job?" He then outlined the requirements of divine care for the entire world.

Job chapters 38–40 offer a tour de force presentation of God's power, told from the perspective of God Himself. God's monolog through these three chapters expressed a majesty and power that doesn't fit in our human frame of reference.

If you want to change your view of God, stop for a moment and read these three chapters. God was rebuking Job for his presumption of arguing on behalf of God. Job's knowledge of God, His power, His plans, and His motivations was so pathetic that it was an act of great arrogance to tell his friends what God was trying to do or accomplish.

Only God could understand His entire plan. He did not need anyone to speak on His behalf or defend Him. He could take care of Himself.

Upon hearing God's rebuke, Job immediately repented.

> Therefore I have uttered what I did not understand,
> things too wonderful for me, which I did not know.
>
> Job 42:3

He knew he had spoken out of turn and was guilty of arrogance. His last response was, "from now on, I'll ask questions, but let You answer them."

Throughout this time of suffering, Job's only sin was presuming to speak for God–something of which he had no actual knowledge. At no time did he accuse God of being unfair to him. Nor did his faith and focus on God waver throughout the ordeal.

Satan lost the wager. Job did not turn against God.

God's response was to restore Job to his former position. God gave him even greater wealth and a new family to replace everything he lost.

In Job, we see the great lesson that our place is to submit to the great and powerful God. We cannot explain Him away. We cannot put Him in a box where we think we have Him figured out. Our task is to accept what He brings into our lives and be thankful for every circumstance.

Psalms–The Heart Relates to God through Music

The Psalms have been called the hymnal of the Hebrews. The book in our Bible contains 150 songs that were sung in the worship of God. It seems reasonable to expect that they were compositions that were sung by choirs in the majestic Temple that Solomon built.

The Psalms give voice to a wide range of emotions and the circumstances behind them. Often, we like to sing songs of God's goodness. But the Psalms are honest in that they faithfully express our hearts in all different times of our life.

- Laments or petitions for God to intervene (Psalm 3, 51)
- Thanksgiving or praise to God (Psalm 30, 65)
- Trust in God (Psalm 4)
- Hymns - Songs about God and His glory (Psalm 47)
- Teaching and wisdom (Psalm 1, 119)

The book of Psalms is a composition from many composers. While David was called "the sweet psalmist of Israel", he did not write all the Psalms. Throughout the book, we see many poetic expressions attributed to many original artists.

That the Bible includes a songbook gives meaning to the command "Make a joyful noise to the Lord". Music has always been a part of the worship of God. And by including a book of songs, we understand how much God values our songs as expressions of our worship to Him.

The Psalms offer redemption for our bleakest days, knowing that we are not alone and that there is a way to share hard times with God. As the psalmists poured out their hearts in the middle of their most difficult times, so, too, can we reach out to God when our perspective seems dark and unforgiving.

David wrote Psalm 3 as he ran from his son Absalom, who had usurped the throne.

David also wrote Psalm 51 as he repented of his sin with Bathsheba and the death of their son.

The Psalms guide us toward wisdom as they direct our emotions toward God. They show that no topic or subject is beneath God's concern. We can pour out our heart to God during any trial that might come our way.

The wise person who truly fears God orients their life toward Him so that when trouble or rejoicing comes, their natural response is to turn to God and share what is happening. There is no sense of "I have to work it out first." Our frustration and our joy are equally welcome in the psalmist's expression.

The Psalms teach us we should set our affections upon God. This isn't because we'll get something back. Often, the cry for relief finds the answer that justice will eventually happen, but maybe not during our lives. We share with God because He is in control. When we remember we are crying out to the Maker of the universe, we can finally rest in His decision and His promise to deliver justice without fail.

We may not get the closure we desire. But we rest knowing that God is God, and that He is good.

> Oh, taste and see that the LORD is good! Blessed is the man who takes refuge in him!
>
> Psalm 34:8

Proverbs–Wisdom Nuggets

Solomon wrote the book of Proverbs. When he ascended to the throne of Israel, God asked him what he most wanted. Solomon asked for wisdom to govern God's great people.

God granted him wisdom, and he became the wisest man who has ever lived. He distilled much of that wisdom into little bite-sized statements in the Proverbs.

> The fear of the LORD is the beginning of wisdom, and the knowledge of the Holy One is insight.
>
> Proverbs 9:10

From his unique position of insight into how to live in a way that pleased God, Solomon shared his collection of wise statements. Solomon did not write the book of Proverbs to tell a story, but to impart wisdom to the reader. It explains how we should live our lives.

The Proverbs always draw us back to God. Just as the fear of God is the beginning, our challenge is to keep that fear and awe and respect central to our lives. As soon as we shift our focus away from God, we leave the path of wisdom and begin living under our power and insight. Since we neither create nor design anything of significance, our wisdom, living a life that pleases us, will only end poorly.

Ecclesiastes–the Meaning of Life

Solomon also wrote the book of Ecclesiastes. He was fabulously wealthy and powerful. With that wealth, he could do whatever he wanted. Curious about human experience, he tested and explored the boundaries of living.

Throughout the book Solomon repeated the phrase "Vanity of vanities, all is vanity!" The word "vanity" occurs repeatedly. We might think of it as "being vain or puffed up," but the meaning is the opposite. When he wrote "vanity", Solomon was referring to something insignificant or insubstantial. It meant something that wasn't even worthy of discussion.

Throughout the book of Ecclesiastes, Solomon shared how he had explored every diversion under the sun. Every time he thought he found a meaningful or enjoyable experience, he had to conclude that it was vanity–insignificant, unable to bring meaning or purpose to his life.

The book of Ecclesiastes hinges on the conclusion that Solomon shared in chapter 12.

> The end of the matter all has been heard. Fear God and keep his commandments, for this is the whole duty of man.
>
> Ecclesiastes 12:13

None of the subjects that Solomon had explored amounted to enough substance to be worth recommending. The only thing that Solomon identified as worthy was to "fear God and keep His commandments."

If we read all but the last few verses of the book of Ecclesiastes, we might think of Ecclesiastes as a book of futility, one that finds no purpose or value in any endeavor. Instead, as we consider the entire book, we see that without God, life has no meaningful purpose. Only in God do we find the value that transcends our existence.

If we want to end our lives well, then we will follow the wise advice of fearing and obeying God to the end of our days. This is the sign of a life well-lived.

Song of Solomon–Courtship and Love in Relationships

On the heels of Solomon's conclusion that we must fear God because all else is insubstantial, we read the Song of Solomon. In this book, Solomon shares his wise thoughts on relationships and how to conduct them well.

Ever since Genesis 2, when God declared he created people for relationships, the desire for has driven us together. While it is possible to live outside of marriage, the common expression of desire is for a life shared with others.

Song of Solomon paints a picture of love expressed between a man and a woman, told through the voice of the woman. It places a high value on the love and romantic longing between men and women that leads to marriage. Just as God sanctified marriage in Genesis 2, the Song of Solomon gives expression to the emotions that lead to marriage.

Gospel Application

These five books nestled in the middle of the Bible are more than "the collection of misfits that don't belong anywhere else." Today, more than ever, we need to be reminded of the divine definition of "the Good Life."

Our culture tries to offer counterfeit pictures of what a good life looks like. These range from overtly hedonistic, "get what you can and enjoy it for all it's worth", to moralistic "follow the golden rule" to the idealistic "just love everyone."

But none of the world's definitions of the "good life" include God. Nor do these ideals present the idea that our life is to revolve around anyone besides ourselves.

In the wisdom literature, we see that a life oriented toward God is the only good life we can pursue. Anything oriented around us leads to vanity and futility and insignificance. We gain a perspective of God as greater than ourselves and not something we can place in any box we desire. Our faith in

Him is just that–Faith in Him. We cannot substitute that faith for knowledge, or it ceases to be faith.

God must capture and hold our attention. Whether we are debating with skeptics or expressing our frustration at the proliferation of evil in the world, we must remain oriented toward God. He gets to decide what happens and what does not. His sense of justice is enough for us. We accept Him and trust in Him.

For us today who have seen Jesus and the picture of God, we have a double assurance of wisdom. Jesus did not fight for what was rightfully His. He did not receive full vindication in the moment of injustice. He suffered affliction in a way that we, as humans, cannot fully understand. Yet He went through with it and kept His focus on God, faithfully remaining obedient to God's plan.

We've seen what it looks like. As we read the Wisdom in the Middle, we should remember Jesus and the example He has already given us.

6

GOD'S SPOKESMEN

ISAIAH - MALACHI

Following the wisdom books in the middle of our Bibles, we come to one of the largest sections–the Prophets. This section begins with Isaiah and ends with Malachi. Seventeen books fall into this category. But, given their titles, these books might not be exactly what you would expect.

In modern times, the word prophecy has taken on a different meaning than what it had when these books were written. Today we think of prophecy as predicting the future. That is not at all the aim of this section of our Bible. Sometimes the prophets spoke of predictions, but that is not the main purpose of this section of the Bible.

The Three Offices

The prophetic books gained this title because men labeled as "prophets" wrote them. This is a special role created by God as part of His relationship with humanity. It's one of three such roles that we see in the Bible. To better understand prophets, we need to consider all three of the roles God instituted.

The First Office: Priest

The purpose of the Priestly office was to make intercession on behalf of the people to God. God appointed them to serve in the Tabernacle (and later the Temple) and they had the duty to make all offerings on behalf of God's people.

Out of all the tribes of Israel, God selected the descendants of Levi to be His special servants. They became the tribe of priests whose job was to manage the tabernacle or the temple and represent the people of Israel before God. Theirs was the exclusive privilege of offering sacrifices to God.

1 Samuel 13 tells the story of King Saul choosing to present an offering for strength in battle because Samuel, the designated priest, was late to their meeting. When he arrived, Samuel told Saul that he had behaved foolishly and disobediently. Even though he was the king, he did not have the right to sacrifice to God.

Once every year, the High Priest entered the Holy of Holies and presented a sacrifice on behalf of the entire nation of Israel. Only the High Priest could perform this service, and only on this specific day. No other priests could enter before God in this way.

The priest represented the people of Israel before God. Only he could make offerings to cover (but not pay for) their sins. No one else could operate the Tabernacle or Temple. Only the High Priest could step into the holiest place and offer the sacrifice of atonement. There was no other way in the

Old Testament to approach God, outside of the office of Priest.

The Second Office: King

The purpose of the King was to rule over and govern the people of God on behalf of God. When God promised Abram, Isaac, and Jacob that He would be their God and they would be His people, He established a relationship of authority over them. Throughout the years that followed, God guided them Himself. When the people needed more direct guidance, God appointed leaders and judges who provided the guidance necessary to resolve a specific problem.

The judges were never permanent leaders. They came only as necessary and often led for the rest of their lives. But the position was not hereditary and often the people rebelled against the children of a Judge (Samuel and Gideon were two good examples).

However, in 1 Samuel 8, we read as the people came to Samuel and demanded that he give them a King. This would allow them to follow the practices of the kingdoms around them and create a more visible source of authority and leadership than God.

In 1 Samuel 8:7, God identified this desire as a rejection of His authority.

> And the LORD said to Samuel, "Obey the voice of the people in all that they say to you, for they have not

> rejected you, but they have rejected me from being king over them."

Later in that same chapter, we read God instructed Samuel to select a king for them. Even though Samuel did what God instructed, it was God Himself who created the office of the King. God granted divine authority to the king to be the ruler of the people God had chosen for Himself. The people were not the king's–they were God's. But the king had the responsibility and privilege of governing them on behalf of God.

As we discovered in the chapter, Long Live the King! Most of the kings who reigned failed to rule justly on behalf of God. All the kings of Israel were wicked and rejected God. All but eight of the kings of Judah were also wicked and perverted the authority God had given them.

The Third Office: Prophet

The last office fell to the people through whom God delivered messages to His people. In the Old Testament, God did not speak personally and privately to individual people. He chose a person to be his spokesperson, and that person arrived on the scene to proclaim, "Thus says the Lord!"

Not all the prophets wrote books in the Bible. In the book of Judges, we read of Deborah, who served as both a prophet and a judge. In the book of 2 Samuel, we learn of Nathan the prophet who advised David the king.

The prophet's responsibility was to repeat in the hearing of the people precisely what they heard from God. They were not to add their interpretation or opinions to what God wanted them to say. In Deuteronomy 18, Moses laid down the standards and expectations for a Prophet.

- If a prophet spoke "a word from God," but it didn't come from God, the person's life was forfeit.
- If a prophet spoke "a word from God," but it did not come true, the prophet was false.

One aspect of the prophetic duty was to speak of things that were to come, what we might think of as "prophecy" today. But that was a small part of their communication. More commonly, the prophets expressed God's opinion of what was going on in the world and served as the voice of God's judgment.

A Look at the Prophets

In our Bibles, there are seventeen books in the prophetic section. A man who delivered God's messages to the people wrote each of these books. These prophets differed from Nathan and Deborah in that someone wrote their words and preserved them for us.

We can divide the books of the prophets into two sub-sections.

The Major Prophets, who wrote the longest of the prophetic books (for example, the book of Isaiah contains 66 chapters)

The Minor Prophets–who wrote shorter prophetic books.

The Major/Minor distinction has no bearing on the impact or importance of the messages in the books, just their length.

Some prophetic books are a collection of many prophetic messages. Isaiah and Jeremiah even identify different sections which address different audiences throughout their book. This made their books more of a compilation of prophetic declarations over a long period.

Jonah is a different type of prophecy book. It tells the story of one episode of Jonah's life. God commanded him to give a single prophetic message to the city of Nineveh (the capital of the Assyrian empire). In it, we find a retelling of the story leading up to and following the delivery of that message.

Historically, the Prophets spanned a long period. Many of them lived and ministered during the time of the Kings of Israel and Judah. Here, they were contemporaries of the stories that we read in the books of Kings and Chronicles.

Other Prophets were called exilic prophets. They lived during the time of the exile in Babylon and their works spoke of God's sovereignty over the conquering nations and a promise that God would not forget his people. Daniel is an example of a prophet during the Exile.

Finally, some prophets lived during the time after the exile when the Jews had returned to their land and rebuilt it. Malachi is the last of these prophets and wrote around 400 BC, several generations after the first wave of people returned under the leadership of Zerubabel.

Throughout the books of prophecy, we see common themes being communicated. God's message was consistent, and He spoke the same general words whenever the people fell into patterns of disobedience.

The Prophets Declared God's Standards and the Consequence of Ignoring Them

As God's people forgot about Him, they needed frequent reminders of who He was and what He expected. A common message of the prophets was to declare God to the people so they would know and change their behavior.

The verses below are illustrations of the kinds of messages that the Prophets communicated on behalf of God.

Nahum 1:2-8–The prophet Nahum spoke to the people of Nineveh (the same ones to which Jonah preached) and painted a picture of God and His anger over the wickedness that He saw in Assyria. In this passage, we see the picture of a righteous God, wrapped in His holiness, meting out judgment against those who do evil.

Amos 2:2-6–Amos, a fig-picker by trade, spoke the words of God to the people of Judah and Israel, promising them punishment for their offenses against Him. He listed their specific transgressions and declared that judgment was coming. Israel and Judah were not the only recipients of these prophetic words, the Prophets communicated punishment on many nations.

Hosea 4:1-3–God reminded the Children of Israel that He opposed their wicked living. Verse three describes the consequences which God had rolled out upon them because of what He saw in their lifestyles and choices. Throughout prophetic literature, we see this picture of sin and punishment again and again.

Joel 2:12-17–The prophet Joel passionately called out to God's people to repent, turn their backs on their wicked ways, and return to a life of obedience to God's law. While God delivered punishment, His heart was for His people to return to Him and rely upon His protection and power.

Zephaniah 2:1-3–Zephaniah delivers the message, "Repent or suffer judgment." Like the message of repentance in Joel 2, this passage focused on the judgment that would occur if repentance did not happen. This was a hard "hellfire and brimstone" demand to the people from a righteous and angry God who could not overlook the offenses against Him.

The prophetic books deliver the message of Romans 6:23 in bold language: The wages of sin is death. The prophets had to communicate a very stern message to the surrounding people of God's displeasure in their choices and their lifestyle.

In return, the people oppressed many of the prophets who delivered God's word to them. Tired of hearing such condemning language, the people struck back at the messenger, trying to silence the words they did not want to hear. Being called to the office of the Prophet was a great blessing, but it came with very real consequences and negative effects as well.

The Prophets Declared God's Faithfulness and Love

Not all the prophetic messages dealt with sin and punishment. Often, God would remind the Children of Israel of His love and dedication to them.

Hosea 3:1-5–Throughout the book of Hosea, the prophet himself plays out the relationship between God and the nation of Israel. Commanded to marry an unfaithful woman, Hosea represented God, who loved a people who were not faithful to Him. Yet, again and again, Hosea acted lovingly toward his wife, who had turned to prostitution and given herself to many men. In the same way, God continued to love His people. He never cast them aside, even though their behavior toward Him was terrible.

Micah 4:1-8–Micah declared God's intent to return to Jerusalem and re-establish Zion as His holy seat. Spoken to a group of disorganized and scattered people, this would have come across as a great declaration. It would have been encouraging to know that God had not given up on them as a people and that God had not forgotten the great promises He made to them.

Jeremiah 31:27-33–A promise to change their hearts and institute a new agreement that would bring God into a direct relationship with them–not through the three offices. Looking at the difficulty of relating to God through the Law, God promised a future change that would cause a softening of their hearts from stone to flesh.

God neither forgot nor abandoned His people. He loved them even as they rebelled against Him and ran from Him. His one-sided commitment to Abraham, Isaac, and Jacob bound Him to them and nothing they could do would break His affection for them.

The Prophets Declared God's Plan to Send a Savior

Every year at Christmas, the Prophets come into focus. Their bold words promising a Messiah in Bethlehem remind us of God's plan of salvation.

Isaiah 9:6-7–This is the promise of a child who would fulfill the promise to David of an eternal King. Unlike all the earthly kings, this king would rule with righteousness and justice.

Micah 5:2–Micah gets very specific and reveals the city where the coming King would be born.

Isaiah 53:1-12–Isaiah spoke of a suffering servant. This promise concerns One who would come and receive the judgment of God upon Himself. We see this as a prophetic foretelling of the life of Jesus who came to live righteously but die a sinner's death.

Zechariah 14:1-9–We read of the coming of the Day of the Lord. This is the day when God comes again in power and might and defeats all who would oppose Him. This Day of the Lord is the day for which all faithful Children of Israel waited in anticipation. They longed for their King to be the mighty One who would subdue all oppressors and opponents and return them to their place in His favor.

God did not get lost in the wickedness of His people. Throughout this time, He remembered His greater plan to bring a Savior and regain the dominion over the earth that He created. At the right times, He shared that message through His prophets and they delivered the news to God's people.

Gospel Application

The prophets represented God's direct communication to His people. Their role was to speak on behalf of God to say what He wanted His people to hear. But hearing the word of

God was never enough to fulfill the promise in Genesis three.

While the prophets delivered the messages God gave them, the people who heard the message often ignored them or even persecuted them for what they had to say. The people did not listen to them. The messages fell on deaf ears and hard hearts.

The prophets show us that redemption could not come through hearing divine instructions. The human condition of sin resisted the influence of God's words. For the people to receive God's word, a much more fundamental shift had to happen.

The prophet Ezekiel puts it very well.

> And I will give you a new heart, and a new spirit I will put within you. And I will remove the heart of stone from your flesh and give you a heart of flesh.
>
> Ezekiel 36:26

The core issue was in the heart of the hearers. Their hearts were hard and therefore not receptive to the words of God. For anything meaningful or permanent to happen, the people would require new hearts.

Despite the unwillingness to hear and respond, we see God's character loud and clear through the prophets. He declared His opposition to sin and promised to reward faithful living. Since God has not changed, we know that the same holds for us today.

INTRODUCTION TO THE NEW TESTAMENT

PART 2

After the Old Testament comes the New Testament. As the name implies, it contains newer works than the Old Testament. We find 27 individual books in the New Testament.

The major theme of the New Testament is the gospel. Simply put, the gospel is the good news that Jesus satisfied the demands of the law, living a perfect life, then exchanged His earned righteousness for our sin and paid the penalty for that sin. Because of Jesus' sacrifice, we no longer need to cover up sin, pending a future ultimate solution. We receive forgiveness for our sin.

A major feature of the New Testament is the introduction of the church. After the four books which tell of Jesus' life, all the remaining books address the church. Jesus promised to build a church that would withstand the worst attacks of the devil. In many of the New Testament books, we find those attacks being repelled and right living explained.

Whereas the Old Testament featured God's people defined by their heritage, the New Testament focuses on God's people defined by their faith. These new people spanned geographical and ethnic boundaries, creating a new people of God where anyone could join through faith.

Much of the New Testament is concerned with grace. This is the teaching that we receive unearned favor from God because of Jesus' sacrifice. There is no act that we can repay God for the grace we have received. Our only action is to receive it gratefully and let it change our outlook on life.

Throughout the New Testament, we read of people who struggled with the gospel and with grace. The early Christians fell prey to into false teaching that polluted the simplicity of the gospel. Whether it was false teachers trying to add extra requirements or inappropriate reliance on grace that led to unholy living, much of the New Testament offers corrections to the errors that had crept into the church.

It wasn't until after Jesus rose again and ascended into Heaven that the books of the New Testament appeared. The earliest books may have been written as early as the 50s AD and the last books in the mid-90s AD. The selection of the books to be included was based on their being written by the apostles or close associates of the apostles, and books that were commonly accepted by the church as authoritative and Holy Spirit guided.

7

THE LIFE AND TIMES OF JESUS THE CHRIST

THE GOSPELS OF MATTHEW, MARK, LUKE AND JOHN

As we continue through the Bible, we come to the Gospels next. These are the books of the Bible that deal directly with the life of Jesus. Stepping back to look at the entire Bible, the Gospels fall into the generic category of "History." In this respect, these four books are like Genesis, Judges, and 2 Chronicles. However, because they uniquely deal with the life of Jesus, we group the gospels into a special category of their own.

From a timeline perspective, the gospels follow the prophetic and historical books of the Old Testament. Ezra and Nehemiah address the events of the fifth century BC. Malachi, the last prophet, received his messages from God in the fourth century BC.

And then there were four hundred years of silence.

This was the longest pause in God's communication since the covenant with Abraham. Undoubtedly, the Jewish leaders felt worry as they tried to understand why God had gone quiet. Had He forgotten them? Had they driven Him away?

Into this tension came Jesus of Nazareth. God didn't choose to speak through a prophet, priest, or king as He had in the past. This time He sent His Son.

What is a Gospel?

The word "gospel" simply means "good news". It could be good news of any kind. "The ice cream truck is in the neighborhood and is giving out free samples" could be good news if you like ice cream and the day is hot. But in this case, the good news centers on God sending Jesus to pay the price for our sin and redeem us back to God.

In scripture, we reserve the term gospel for the four books which tell the story of Jesus. Jesus Himself is God's good news. He was the fulfillment of the promise God made back in Genesis 3, telling us that God would one day break Satan's power. Jesus was the ultimate Passover Lamb, completing the picture that was started in Exodus. He came as the perfect Prophet who could speak on behalf of God. He was the perfect Priest, who could offer the ultimate sacrifice that would forgive sins once and for all. He was the ultimate King of the line of David, who will one day sit on the throne and rule forever.

The Old Testament was looking forward to the coming of Jesus. Whether the writers or the people they wrote to knew it or not, Jesus was the one who would make everything right with God. Their faith was confidence that someday God would do something that would address sin and make permanent all the temporary cover-ups that they had been using.

For this reason, we call these four books the "good news." They tell us of the greatest news of all.

Meet the Gospel Writers

We have four different gospel accounts in our Bible. They contain a lot of overlap. But each one targeted a different audience and communicated different aspects of Jesus' life and ministry.

The accounts written by Matthew, Mark, and Luke are called the "synoptic gospels." Synoptic means "same viewpoint" or "same view". And as we read in our Bible, we can see that these books all follow a similar chronological narrative style of telling the story of Jesus. The gospel of John stands alone as the non-synoptic account and uses a more thematic structure.

Matthew

Written by Matthew Levi, the former tax collecting disciple of Jesus, this book appeals to a Jewish audience. Matthew gives a lot of attention to matters that would have interested his fellow Jews who were familiar with the law and the prophets. Much of the material in the book brings focus to Jesus' fulfillment of prophecy and His claim to be the Chosen One, the Messiah.

Mark

John Mark was a friend of Peter, and possibly a part of the larger crowd of people who followed Jesus. During his account of Jesus' betrayal and arrest, he mentions a young man fleeing naked from the scene. Some scholars believe he was referring to himself.

Mark's book addresses a Roman audience. His account is the shortest of the four gospels and follows a literary style that is much more oriented around the action. The word "immediately" appears over forty times in his book–emphasizing events happening one after another.

Luke

Luke was a Greek physician and companion of the Apostle Paul. A Greek named Theophilus (which roughly translates into "Lover of God") asked him to tell the story of Jesus. Luke did not witness any of the events firsthand, but says that he carefully researched everything he wrote and interviewed the people who were there. Correspondingly, his account focuses on a Greek audience.

John

John, the beloved disciple of Jesus, wrote a very different account of Jesus' life. While his composition has a unique structure, it agrees with and supports the other accounts. At the end of the book, John describes his purpose in writing the account.

> But these are written so that you may believe that Jesus is the Christ, the Son of God, and that by believing you may have life in his name. John 20:31

John wrote his gospel to convince people to believe in Jesus. He organized his work around seven major miracles, seven major discourses or talks, and seven major "I AM" statements made by Jesus.

A Summary of the Four Gospels

There are many ways that we could summarize the four gospels. We could attempt to do it culturally or thematically, or based on Jesus' teaching. Here I will offer a roughly chronological listing of major events that happened in the life of Jesus, building to the climax of all four of the accounts.

Jesus Before Creation

John 1:1-18

John started the story of Jesus' life long before the nativity scene in Bethlehem. John declared Jesus existed with God before the creation of the world. His opening words "In the beginning..." echo those of Moses in Genesis 1.

He was in the beginning with God. (John 1:2)

John said that Jesus existed before God created anything. He was one with God the creator, not part of the created universe. John didn't beat around the bush. In the first verses of his book, he declared Jesus was the eternal God.

John states Jesus played a part in the process of creation (John 1:3). Not a minor role or an assisting role, but an essential role. Without Jesus in the beginning, the world we know would not have come into existence.

As we continue to read through the events of His earthly life, John wanted us to remember that Jesus' story didn't start in Bethlehem.

The Miraculous Birth

Matthew 1-2, Luke 2

Every Christmas we return to these beloved passages about the babe in a manger and no room at the inn. We love the shepherds and the wise men and the angelic choir singing "Glory to God in the highest."

The gospels of Matthew and Luke tell us that Jesus was not an ordinary baby conceived the ordinary way. Jesus was born of Mary, but not of Joseph. He was fully human, but also fully God.

We receive very little information about His childhood. He understood early on that His purpose and mission were from above and that His Heavenly Father had work for Him to accomplish. We don't know when the reality of the cross came to Him. But He knew He had a purpose.

John Announces Jesus

Matthew 3, Luke 3

John the Baptist was Jesus' second cousin. The gospel of Mark identifies John as "one crying in the wilderness, 'Make straight the paths of the Lord.'" He had a specific role in announcing Jesus and introduce Jesus to the people, as foretold by the prophet Isaiah.

John made quite a splash in his day. He lived in the wilderness, wore austere clothing, and ate insects and honey. People from all over flocked to hear him, wondering if He was the promised one. When he started baptizing the people who declared their repentance, it primed the crowds for something great to happen.

John's ministry was one of preparation. He called the people to repent. He could not offer forgiveness. His job was to make the people aware of their sins and properly sorrowful, so they could receive Jesus as God intended.

The pinnacle of John's ministry happened when he baptized Jesus. Jesus didn't come to John to repent, since He had never sinned and had nothing to repent of. He came to be announced by John, acknowledged by God the Father and the Holy Spirit.

Satan Tempts Jesus

Matthew 4, Luke 4

Immediately after His baptism, Jesus retreated into the wilderness where He spent forty days fasting and preparing for His earthly ministry. At the end of this period, while weak with hunger, Satan came to Him and tempted Him with a variety of short-cuts.

In the first temptation, Satan suggested Jesus use His divine power for personal benefit. Satan knew He was hungry and said simply, "turn these rocks into bread and eat." But that would have been a perversion of God's plan and would have disqualified Him from completing His sinless substitutionary sacrifice.

Satan's second attempt was to get Jesus to use His divine powers to make His ministry easier. By throwing Himself off the top of the temple and being rescued by angels, Jesus would have impressed the crowd at the Temple. They would have gladly installed Him as their new King. But Jesus knew his purpose was to be the suffering sacrifice, not the triumphant King.

In the third temptation, Satan offered a simple trade. From the very beginning, Satan wanted to be equal with God. If Jesus would worship him, essentially declaring him the same as God the Father, Satan would relinquish dominion over all humanity and give it to Jesus. But this was not God's plan and would have violated God's holy character.

In each of these temptations, Jesus used the word of God to rebuke Satan. He did not give in to the apparent ease of a shortcut, but relied upon God to know the best way to accomplish what needed to be done.

Jesus Launches His Public Ministry

Matthew 4, Luke 4, Mark 1

After resisting Satan's temptations, Jesus began His public ministry. He called His disciples and visited many cities in the northern region of Galilee, preaching, and performing miracles of healing and exorcism.

Throughout this phase of His ministry, Jesus had one overarching message. "Repent for the Kingdom of God is at hand." In this message, He continued John the Baptist's call to repentance. Ultimately, He wanted a change of heart for the people and that began with acknowledging their sin and turning from it.

During this part of His ministry, Jesus showed His authority over sickness, demons, and the natural world. His miracles declared his power. He was the King of kings, and He was there in their midst. His kingdom existed wherever His power was on display.

The Discussion with Nicodemus

John 3

One of Jesus' most famous conversations was with a man named Nicodemus who was a Pharisee, and a member of the Jewish governing council. Nicodemus came to Jesus secretly by night. He did not want any of his colleagues to hear that he had been talking to Jesus, because the Jewish leaders had already developed an antagonistic relationship with Him.

Nicodemus wanted to know who Jesus was and how He did all the miracles. He said that the Pharisees knew there was something special about Jesus because of the miracles. But where the Pharisees wanted to control Jesus, Nicodemus wanted what Jesus offered.

Jesus steered the conversation in a spiritual direction and talked to Nicodemus about being "born again" as the way to see and experience the kingdom of God. This confused Nicodemus and he tried to puzzle out how he could physically be reborn.

Jesus clarified it wasn't a physical birth He was talking about. It was a spiritual second birth. Nicodemus was spiritually dead and if he wanted to see the kingdom of God, he would need to be born into spiritual life.

This discussion gives us perhaps the most famous and well-known verse in the Bible.

> For God so loved the world, that he gave his only Son, that whoever believes in him should not perish but have eternal life.
>
> John 3:16

Rejected by the Jewish Leaders

Matthew 12:14-37

Throughout His early ministry, Jesus drew the attention of the Jewish leaders in Jerusalem. They sent a delegation to observe and see if the stories of miracles were true. As Jesus' authority over demons and disease became obvious, they questioned Him about what He was doing and where His power came from.

The relationship between Jesus and the Pharisees was tense from the beginning. He saw how they abused their power and used it for their benefit. He publicly called them "a brood of vipers," "white-washed tombs," and "children of the devil."

The more Jesus amazed the crowds, the more He put the Pharisees in a tight spot. The uneducated crowd expected the Pharisees to decide whether Jesus was the Messiah. If they said, "He is the Messiah," then they would have to submit to His harsh words concerning their sin and hypocrisy. If they said, "He isn't the Messiah," then the crowd would expect an explanation that accounted for all the miracles.

This tension came to a head in Matthew 12. Jesus had just cast out a demon. The crowd was astonished at this, and asked, "Is He the Messiah?"

The Pharisees, who were there and heard this question, finally offered their answer.

"This was all a show designed to trick you," they said. "He is not the Messiah. He uses the power of the devil to cast out demons."

The Pharisees, as the leaders of Israel, had rendered their verdict. They had declared that Jesus was not the Messiah. Despite ample miraculous evidence, Jesus did not fit their picture of how the Messiah would act. Unable to explain His power in any other way, they described His miracles as satanic.

This must have come as a shock to the people who heard it. Jesus seemed to be from God, not Satan. But with this decision, they put the matter to rest. The Pharisees backed up their shocking announcement with their full authority as the leaders of the people, and no one dared to defy them.

Jesus chastised them and told them that what they had just done was blasphemy against the Spirit of God. For this sin, they would not receive forgiveness. They could not undo the decision they just shared.

For this reason, John wrote in the introduction to his Gospel:

> He came to his own, and his own people did not receive him.
>
> John 1:11

Jesus Teaches in Parables

Following this encounter with the Pharisees and their rejection of His authority and His power, Jesus changed His ministry approach. After this point, we no longer hear His usual appeal about repenting because the Kingdom of God was nearby. From this point on, Jesus hid what He was trying to say from the crowds around Him.

Starting in Matthew 13, Jesus began teaching in parables. Some might say that parables are folksy tales meant to appeal to a broad audience. Both the disciples and Jesus both disagree with this interpretation.

After telling His first parable, the disciples came to Jesus and asked why He was talking to the people that way. They did not know what He was trying to say. They didn't understand the parable or its hidden message.

Jesus answered, "To you, it has been given to know the secrets of the kingdom of heaven, but to them [the crowds], it has not been given." (Matthew 13:11)

Jesus was speaking in parables to hide His meaning from the people who would not leave Him alone. Later, He explained the meaning of the parables privately to His disciples. His people had rejected Him. His message was no longer to them.

The parables Jesus taught His disciples (but not the crowds) explained different aspects of the Kingdom of God. Earlier, He had been preaching to the people that the Kingdom was nearby. Now He was telling His disciples how to understand what the Kingdom was.

For the rest of the Gospel accounts, Jesus worked with His disciples to prepare them for what was to come. He knew His time would be short and then He would have to leave them. This was the intensive class on how to believe in Him.

Jesus Introduces the Church

Matthew 16:13-20

After the change of ministry strategy, Jesus took His disciples out into the countryside. There, He asked a big question.

"Who do people say that I am?"

His disciples repeated back what they had heard in the towns of Galilee. A teacher. A prophet. John the Baptist raised from the dead.

"Who do you say I am?"

In what may have been Peter's finest moment, he blurted out, "You are the Christ (which is the Greek translation of Messiah), the Son of the living God."

Jesus affirmed what Peter had said and said that Peter's confession was a tiny piece (a pebble) of a much larger thing (a rock or boulder). And upon that rock, Jesus said He would build His church. Grounded upon this great confession of faith, all the powers of Hell would not prevail against it.

This was the first time that Jesus had spoken about something much bigger than the faithful group that followed Him around the Galilean countryside. Though they probably didn't understand what He was talking about, that understanding probably came later when the church sprang into existence.

The Triumphal Entry

Matthew 21:1-11; Mark 11:1-11; Luke 19

Before the third Passover of His public ministry, Jesus headed into Jerusalem. This decision distressed His disciples tremendously. The tensions with the Jewish authorities had become so bad they expected they were all going to their deaths. Normally, they stayed up in Galilee and out of the political limelight. But Jesus was determined to celebrate the Passover in Jerusalem, regardless of what the consequences might be.

As He approached Jerusalem, word of His arrival spread ahead of Him. The capital city was bursting with people who celebrating the Passover festival. Only at the temple could they sacrifice their Passover lambs. Every Jewish family that could afford it had come up to Jerusalem.

The crowd rushed out to see Jesus. They remembered His miracles and His power. With a king who could feed multitudes from a few bits of food, they could overthrow off the Romans and establish a new Jewish kingdom.

They worshipped Him, crying out "Hosanna!" and paved His path with palm fronds and the cloaks off their backs. Jesus knew their adoration would not last. They had already rejected Him once and would do so again in a matter of days.

Once in Jerusalem, Jesus continued to teach publicly in a cat-and-mouse game with the Pharisees and Jewish authorities. The Pharisees feared If He started doing miracles, the enormous crowds would spontaneously acclaim Him as their King. They wanted to arrest Him quietly and remove Him from the scene, but the people loved Jesus and throngs of people always surrounded Him.

The Betrayal and Trial

John 18:12-19:16; Luke 22:63-23:25

When the arrest came, it was at night in a secluded garden outside the walls of Jerusalem. Acting on information received from Judas Iscariot, one of Jesus' disciples, the Jewish leaders brought a squad of soldiers to take Jesus into custody.

The disciples were no match for the soldiers and simply ran away. Jesus submitted to the arrest and resisted no further.

That night, they shuttled him from the home of Annas to the house of his son-in-law Caiaphas and back. These two were sharing the High Priestly duties that year and led the trial, seeking some means to put Him away. In both locations, the Jewish leaders interrogated Jesus and physically assaulted Him.

The next morning, they presented Jesus to Pilate, the Roman Proconsul of Judea. He alone had the authority to sentence Jesus to death. Once again, Jesus bounced from location to location as Pilate tried to pass the political hot potato to Herod, the Jewish ruler, who was also in town. Neither leader found cause to sentence Jesus.

Finally, the Pharisees played their trump card. They told Pilate that if he didn't do as they demanded, they would tell Caesar that Pilate was supporting a rival king. Left no political choice, Pilate issued the death sentence.

The Death and Burial

Matt 27:27-66; John 19:17-42

The Romans liked to make a spectacle out of executing people. They marched Jesus out of the city and nailed to the cross. After the flogging and beating he had received, He couldn't make the journey, and an onlooker had to be conscripted to carry His cross.

At about three PM, Jesus took on the sin of the world and God the Father turned His back on His Son. Jesus cried out, "My God, why have You forsaken Me?" At that moment, the full weight of sin pressed down on Him. Having taken our sin, He cried out, "It is finished." Then He died.

Normally, a crucifixion would be a multi-day affair as the condemned struggled to hang on to life. It was part of the horror of the execution that was meant as a deterrent to anyone who would consider opposing the authority of Rome.

Since the next day was a major Jewish holiday and the Jewish leaders didn't want the dead and dying bodies outside the city while they celebrated the Passover, the Roman soldiers sped up the process so the condemned would die before sundown. It surprised them when they came to Jesus and discovered He was already dead.

The other prisoners were taken down and thrown into a common grave. But a rich man named Joseph of Arimathea petitioned Pilate for Jesus' body. He was a Jewish leader but, like Nicodemus, was a quiet believer in Jesus and wanted to see Him buried properly. Quickly preparing the body, he laid it in his tomb in a pleasant garden.

The Pharisees were worried that desperate disciples would steal the body from the grave and claim it was a miracle. They persuaded Pilate to seal the tomb. Then he stationed a squad of Roman legionnaires to stand guard on the tomb to prevent any mischief.

Resurrection Day

John 20:1-10

But a wax seal and soldiers could not keep Jesus in the grave. On the morning of the third day, God the Father resurrected Him, blowing away the stone from the grave and scattering the soldiers.

The first person to notice was Mary Magdalene. She was hoping to get access to the body so she could finish the burial preparations that she had not finished earlier. When she arrived in the garden to talk to the soldiers, she discovered the grave was open and nobody was there.

She ran back to the place where the disciples were hiding and announced, "He is gone!" Of all the disciples, only Peter and John believed her enough to check out what she had said. They ran back to the tomb and looked in. Then they went back to the others and confirmed Mary's story, but could not explain what had just happened.

Later, Jesus appeared to the disciples. They could talk to Him and verify that it was Him. Thomas missed the first visit. He resolutely declared that there was no way he would believe unless he could put his fingers in the holes in Jesus' hands and feet.

The next time Jesus appeared, Thomas fell to his knees and could only croak out "My Lord and my God."

Jesus Gives His Last Commands

Matt 28:19-20; Mark 16:19-20

Jesus remained with the disciples for 40 days after the resurrection. During this time, He met with them more than once and appeared a large gathering of five hundred people. These were eyewitnesses who could testify to the resurrection should anyone wonder if the story was true.

Finally, Jesus announced the time had come for Him to return to the Father. Back in Galilee, where most of His ministry had occurred, Jesus met with the disciples for the last time. There He delivered His last instructions:

> "All authority in heaven and on earth has been given to me. Go therefore and make disciples of all nations, baptizing them in the name of the Father and of the Son and of the Holy Spirit, teaching them to observe all that I have commanded you. And behold, I am with you always, to the end of the age."

Matthew 28:19-20

This was the end of Jesus' time on Earth. He ascended into Heaven where He now intercedes on behalf of believers and sees to the building of His church.

He will come again. The next time, however, it will not be to proclaim, "The Kingdom of God is near." He will come as the conquering King.

But that's a story for another chapter in this wonderful story of the Bible.

Gospel Application

The gospels declare the good news of God. Rather than sending a priest, a prophet, or a king, God sent His Son.

Jesus lived a perfect life that satisfied God's requirements. But instead of enjoying the benefits of His righteousness, He exchanged it for our sin. When He took our sin, He also took the punishment that came with it.

Jesus did not come to reign as a king. He came as the sacrifice. No one could solve the sin problem through superior leadership. Hebrews 9:22 says, "without the shedding of blood, there is no forgiveness of sins." Jesus came to shed His blood.

This was God's plan from the Garden of Eden. He called out a people and laid His claim on them. He made promises and covenants to them that laid the foundation for His gospel plan. And when the time was right, He sent His Son to be the Savior of the world.

The serpent bruised Jesus' heel by forcing Him to experience sin and death. None of that experience was pleasant. But the power of God overcame death, and it brought Jesus back to life. God Himself broke the serpent's power over humanity. No longer were they bound to him and blocked from a relationship with God. Jesus defeated the power of death and sin and brought a new relationship with God back onto the table.

The Old Testament looked forward to this sacrifice. It was the permanent solution that was superior to all the temporary solutions that were available to them. Old Testament saints were justified based on their faith that God would provide a better way. They believed in God's promise to provide a way, even if they didn't know what it would look like.

Today, we look back on the gospel and benefit from seeing the answer to the problem. But the gospel still demands faith from us. Faith is still the means to engage the gospel. We must have faith that what Jesus did was enough. Faith that the promises of eternal life and access to God are real. Faith that Jesus took the punishment for our sins and we will not have any surprises in the end.

8

THE BIRTH OF THE CHURCH

ACTS PART 1

At the end of the gospels, the resurrected Jesus gave the famous Great Commission to His disciples. "Go and make disciples." He'd spent forty days with them after the resurrection, but the promised Comforter (John 14:16-17) had not come, and He had not yet built His church (Matthew 16:18).

In the book of Acts of the Apostles, we find the fulfillment of both promises.

While the title of this book of the Bible is the Acts of the Apostles, what we see on display is the power of the Holy Spirit manifested through them. The apostles were the human actors, but the Holy Spirit was delivering God's plan for His new redeemed people.

Pentecost–the Church begins with a BANG!

When Jesus ascended into Heaven from Galilee, He sent His disciples back to Jerusalem to wait. He didn't tell them what they were waiting for, or how they would know. He only told them they would see the fulfillment of God's promise, and they would receive the Holy Spirit.

In Acts 1:8, Jesus told the disciples that they would receive power when the Holy Spirit came upon them. As He spoke about this power, the Holy Spirit would bring, He used a word that is related to our word dynamite. The Holy Spirit would come with explosive power. He would transform everything He touched. No one could control or contain Him. He would destroy the old and introduce something new.

The disciples didn't understand this yet. They were in the dark, but the light was coming.

The Jewish holiday of Shavuot (Festival of Weeks) was one of the three pilgrimage holidays for the Jewish people. Falling seven weeks after Passover, it celebrated the conclusion of the wheat harvest. Once again, Jerusalem would have filled to overflowing with Jewish pilgrims who descended upon Jerusalem to celebrate and make their offerings of loaves of bread from the harvest.

It was precisely in this setting that the Holy Spirit came.

Empowered by the Holy Spirit...

Luke, who wrote the book of Acts, did not experience the coming of the Holy Spirit with the rest of the disciples. But he interviewed those who were there. Even with the best research and eyewitness testimony, it seems like Luke struggled to describe what happened.

First came a noise. Luke described it as the sound of a great wind. It filled the ears of everyone gathered in the room together. But the air wasn't moving.

Then came a strange sight. Luke described it with two metaphors, tongues and fire. They conveyed the image of wavering and flickering. There was one for everyone in the room, and these apparitions appeared to settle on each of them.

Not knowing what was going on, this would have been an unnerving series of events. But more was to come as the effects became apparent. The disciples spoke in languages they had not previously learned.

Acts 2:5 reports that God-fearing Jewish people from all over the world filled Jerusalem. Shavuot would have gathered them all together in the city. The sound of the rushing wind drew a crowd. Everyone wondered what was happening.

Acts 2:6 says that the disciples went out to them and preached the gospel, and the crowd heard the good news in their native language. They wondered and marveled at this, remarking that the disciples were ordinary people from Galilee, not sophisticated learned men.

...Peter preached a great sermon...

Peter, in his typical headstrong way, responded to the astonishment and the side claims that they were drunk, stepped forward to tell everyone what was going on.

Verses 14 through 40 of Acts chapter two record Peter's great sermon. He didn't go easy on his audience. Peter didn't apply subtle psychology to convince them of anything. He didn't beat about the bush and wait for them to ask questions. Peter went for the jugular.

He began by explaining what they saw not as drunkenness, but the satisfaction of a prophecy made in the Old Testament (Joel 2:28). The Spirit of God had come and now He dwelt among men and women on Earth.

Then, in so many words, Peter accused them of their sin. He told them that Jesus of Nazareth had come from God, and they had rejected and crucified Him as a common criminal.

God raised Jesus from the dead, and many testified to His resurrection. Through His power, Jesus had paid the penalty for sin and the broke the power of sin–but they had to repent and come out from among the guilty to receive it.

We don't have the entire sermon. Undoubtedly, Peter went on for a long time. He had spent years being prepared by Jesus, and suddenly the pieces were falling into place.

...And the results were staggering!

Acts 2:41 simply says that on the day of Shavuot, later named Pentecost by the church, over three thousand people believed and joined the Church. This speaks to the power of the Holy Spirit. The first time they heard the message, they believed.

Just like that, the church was born. Not only did the people of Jerusalem believe, but so did those pilgrims who had come for the festival. They then returned home and took with them the message of the gospel. In one move, the gospel scattered to the nations.

Faith Spread to the Gentiles

While the first day of the church saw tremendous growth, the apostles limited their outreach to the Jewish population. Only Jews would have come to the city for the festival. Peter tailored his sermon to a Jewish audience. It seemed to make sense to them that this new faith was an extension or continuation of their previous faith.

But the Jews had already rejected Jesus (Matthew 12). His focus in the latter half of His ministry was on His disciples, not His countrymen. This limitation existed in the minds of the apostles, but not in Jesus' plans for His church.

Once again, it fell to Peter to open the door of ministry. While staying in Joppa, on the coast of the Mediterranean Sea, he had a strange dream. In the dream, he saw a banquet of food, none of which he could eat under Jewish dietary law.

The food appeared three times. Each time, Peter refused, clinging to the old prohibitions. Finally, a voice, as of God, spoke to him. "What God has made clean, do not call common (unclean)."

When Peter woke from the dream, he probably did not understand what had just happened. It was a strange dream for sure, but he had no reason to suspect that it was as world-shattering as he would later learn.

Not long after this dream, a messenger informed Peter that some men had arrived to visit him. They wanted to take him to meet a man named Cornelius, who was a Roman centurion. Normally a proper Jew would not visit the home of a Gentile. However, Peter agreed to go and by the time he arrived, he had figured out the meaning of the food vision. Gentiles were no longer to be unclean and avoided.

Cornelius greeted Peter and explained that he, too, had had a dream and that in it he was told to call for Peter to come and reveal a message from God. Even though he was a Gentile, Cornelius had been following the Jewish faith and believed in God. Now there was something more for him, and he wanted to know what it was.

By now, the dream made complete sense to Peter. He understood that Jesus' church wasn't to be a Jewish church, but an international and multi-cultural church. He began preaching another sermon, explaining who Jesus was and what He had done.

The Holy Spirit didn't wait for Peter to finish preaching. In the middle of his sermon, the Spirit fell upon Cornelius and the members of his household and staff, who had gathered to meet Peter. They began speaking other languages, just as the Apostles had.

The Church Grows

Peter had a sales job when he returned to Jerusalem to explain what had happened. Many of the Christians were upset by what he had done. Some accused him of sinning because he had visited a gentile.

Peter had to tell the entire story of his dream and the visitors from Caesarea, who had taken him to Cornelius. When he was done, everyone was speechless.

> When they heard these things, they fell silent. And they glorified God, saying, "Then to the Gentiles also God has granted repentance that leads to life."
>
> Acts 11:18

Not long after, reports from Antioch, a Roman city to the North, arrived in Jerusalem. The gospel had come and people had believed. Once again, the Spirit had exceeded their expectations and shown them that their understanding of Jesus' plan to build the church was too small.

The Apostles sent a man named Barnabas to check out these claims. He traveled to Antioch and verified that it was true. The gospel was spreading.

Beginning in Jerusalem, the church had spread throughout Judea and Samaria and was now entering the "uttermost parts of the Earth." Not only that, but the reach of the gospel was more than Jewish. Gentiles had, against all expectations, responded to the preaching and now were joining the church in ever-growing numbers.

Gospel Application

Where the prophets described the need for hearts of flesh, the book of Acts shows us how that came about. Through the power of the Holy Spirit, God was changing people's lives, and the gospel results transformed lives all over Jerusalem. God was taking away hearts of stone and replacing them with hearts of flesh, just as He had promised through the prophets.

Acts also introduced the church. With Jesus as its head and the Holy Spirit coming upon all who joined, it was a powerful force for the gospel. Not only were lives being changed, but they were being bound through this new creation.

Acts showed that even though individual people received forgiveness for their sins, that didn't mean that they were on their own. They still had a shared future as the people of God, and God intended they would become a part of this new body.

Not only was the church the privilege of those who believed in God, but it was also itself a force for gospel outreach to the people who lived in the surrounding communities. As a people of God in the church, the testimony to the community was a powerful witness.

Nor was the church simply to be a gathering of like-minded individuals. The gospel broke down all previously known barriers of race and culture and brought together people from all different walks of life. Jews, the people of God, blended with gentiles who were previously outsiders. The power of the Holy spirit united everyone.

Such was the power of the gospel. It brought a new heart through the power of the Holy Spirit and created a new people of God based, not family lineage, but on faith.

9

THE SPREAD OF THE CHURCH

ACTS PART 2

So far, in the book of Acts, we've watched the church explode onto the scene, beginning the fulfillment of Jesus' promise in Matthew 16:18. Propelled by the Holy Spirit and His dynamite power, Peter preached a great sermon, and the growth began. Later, the gospel spread to other cities and even to gentiles, with the same dramatic results.

Luke, the writer of Acts, focused on Peter as the key person who took part in these events. However, part-way through the book, he shifted focus to another major figure in the early church: The Apostle Paul.

Saul the Great Persecutor

We first meet Paul as Saul of Tarsus, an up-and-coming Pharisee in the Jewish religious scene, in Acts chapter seven. There we read that when Stephen, the first martyr, was stoned, the people picking up stones laid their cloaks at Saul's feet. (Acts 7:58)

This seems like an odd comment for Luke to make. Our natural assumption might be to think that Saul was the assistant managing the coat closet. It's more likely that he was the one who approved the stoning. By presenting their cloaks, the people formally submitted to his authority. They were signing up to carry out his will.

This interpretation aligns well with the opening of Acts eight. Saul approved of Stephen's execution. His approval was the opening of great persecution against Christians in Jerusalem. The danger was so real that Christians fled the city and settled all over the eastern Mediterranean region.

Saul's Conversion

Acts nine began with Saul "breathing threats and murder against the disciples of the Lord." He wanted to follow the believers beyond the traditional borders of Israel into the city of Damascus (in modern-day Syria). He received orders to take to the leaders of the synagogues there, allowing him to arrest any Christian Jews who still worshipped in the synagogues.

It was on this persecution road trip that Saul met Jesus. Blinded by a bright light, he heard the voice of Jesus. Unable to see, he continued to Damascus, where he waited for Jesus to make the next move. Three days later, God instructed a Christian named Ananias to go to Saul because "he is a chosen instrument of mine to carry my name before the Gentiles and kings and the children of Israel."

Saul believed and received the Holy Spirit. This conversion set his life on a fresh path. Not only did he forsake his commission to harass and persecute believers, but he preached about his conversion.

Saul engaged in the business of his Savior with the same intensity and determination with which he had previously persecuted Jesus. But when he showed up in synagogues to worship and teach, the Jews resisted his message.

"Is not this the man who made havoc in Jerusalem of those who called upon this name? And has he not come here for this purpose, to bring them bound before the chief priests?"

Acts 9:21

Saul could not pivot from Great Antagonist to Great Advocate in one step. He tried to meet with the apostles to tell his story, but they were afraid of him. Not until Barnabas stepped forward to vouch for him was he even able to share his conversion story.

When they finally heard, the Apostles accepted Saul. His conversion was clear to them, just like Cornelius and the church in Antioch. The Jewish community, however, hated Saul and considered his conversion a betrayal. To save his life, they sent him out of the region to his hometown Tarsus (in modern-day Turkey) until the tension calmed down.

Saul spent years preparing for the ministry that would eventually come. In his letter to the Galatians, he states he went away to Arabia for three years before he returned to Jerusalem. In 2 Corinthians chapter 12, Paul speaks indirectly about "a man" who was caught up in the third heaven where he heard "things which cannot be told, which men may not utter." Many scholars believe he was speaking modestly about himself, and his time being instructed by Jesus.

Four great missionary journeys shaped Saul's ministry across the Roman Empire. As he journeyed, he changed his name from the Jewish Saul to the more Roman name Paul. This was in keeping with his mission to preach the story of Jesus to the gentile communities across the Eastern Roman Empire.

The First Missionary Journey

Paul set out with a small team, including Barnabas and John Mark, the author of the gospel of Mark. They left from Antioch and traveled throughout the Roman Province of Asia Minor, which is in modern-day Turkey.

Paul's missionary method was similar in every town. He went to the local synagogue for the dispersed Jewish population. There, he exercised his right to speak and used the scriptures to present the truth about Jesus. Eventually, they would kick him out of the synagogue and would shift to the public spaces and houses of those who believed in what he had taught. In this manner, he also presented to the gentiles in the region. After establishing a house church, he moved on to the next town.

During this journey, Paul aroused such antagonism in his fellow Jews that, that at one point, a mob of his countrymen grabbed him, dragged him outside the city, and stoned him. Through a miracle, God saved Paul's life, and when the mob disbanded, he got up, tended to his injuries, and moved on to the next city.

Over two years, Paul and his team traveled throughout the southern half of the province. At some point, the pressure became too much for John Mark, and he left Paul and Barnabas to return home to Jerusalem. This abandonment made Paul angry, and he would not easily forget John Mark's lack of commitment.

When Paul and Barnabas returned to Antioch, they reported the results of their travels. They had great news of the churches that they had planted, and the disciples and leaders celebrated with them.

During this inter-trip period, a major issue arose in the church regarding the gentile believers. Some leaders wanted to require them to convert to Jewish religious practices as well. This meant circumcision, food purity, and other Jewish rules. A council gathered in Jerusalem to consider the matter.

In Acts 15, we read of this council and the debate that they considered. Peter, remembering his experience with Cornelius, argued that requiring Jewish practices made little sense. Placing the burden of Jewish law on the gentiles, he said, was not realistic, when the Jews themselves could not effectively keep those same laws. The final decision concluded that gentiles did not have to submit to the Jewish law but should flee from the idolatry that the Greek and Roman culture embraced, and to live a pure, moral life.

The Second Missionary Journey

Paul didn't enjoy sitting around. After the council in Jerusalem, he approached Barnabas to undertake a second journey. Barnabas was willing, but wanted to bring John Mark and give him a chance to redeem himself and prove his worth. Paul adamantly refused to take John Mark with, and so the two missionaries parted ways. Barnabas traveled with John Mark, and Paul selected a man named Silas to be his new partner.

The second journey included a return to the churches that Paul had planted on his first trip. They traveled through the region of Galatia and visited many of the churches where Paul had spent time before. Along the way, Timothy, a gentile convert, joined the team.

After visiting the Galatian churches, Paul traveled along the Aegean Sea to the city of Troas. One night Paul had a dream that a man from Macedonia was beckoning him to visit them. Choosing to follow the guidance of the dream, Paul abandoned his earlier plan to travel north and east and turned west toward Macedonia.

Philippi was his first stop, and he converted Lydia, the first recorded European believer. While he was in Philippi, he cast a demon out of a slave girl who told fortunes for money. This so upset her masters that they had Paul whipped and thrown in prison. That night an earthquake shook the city, and the doors of the prison sprang open. Paul and Silas convinced all the prisoners to stay, and when the jailer discovered the prison opened, but no one was missing, he too believed.

The next day, Paul met with the city leaders. He revealed they had violated his rights as a Roman citizen. He wondered what Caesar would say if he heard of the way they had treated Paul. Ashamed for not following due process, the city leaders let him go and sent him on his way.

Paul traveled through the cities of Macedonia and Greece. During this time, he planted churches and met with believers in every city he visited. He wrote many of his letters, which we will consider in the next chapter, to the churches that he planted and nurtured through these missionary journeys.

Paul's Third Missionary Journey

Once again, Paul headed out to visit and encourage the churches and plant new churches. He traveled through the region of Galatia again, ending up in the major metropolis of Ephesus on the western coast of Asia Minor.

Paul remained in Ephesus for three years. He planted a church and spent a long time developing the leaders to oversee such a large church. In later years, Paul wrote a letter to that church and two letters to his protégé, Timothy, who had become the leader there.

Ephesus boasted a magnificent temple to the Roman god Diana. Such was the effectiveness of Paul's ministry in Ephesus, that the number of pilgrims who came to Ephesus to worship Diana declined. The silversmiths, who made small figurines of the goddess Diana, noticed a decline in their income, and under the instigation of a smith named Demetrius rioted in the streets, protesting Paul's influence.

They forced Paul to leave the city after this and he returned to Greece and Macedonia, where he visited the churches that he had planted on the second journey. Most likely, he spent an extended time in Corinth, another large city with a thriving church that needed strong leadership.

Paul at the Mercy of the Jewish Leaders

Paul ended the third missionary journey early when he learned that some of the Jews in Greece were planning to assassinate him. Such was his reputation for preaching Christ and leading Jews out of the synagogue into the Christian churches. The Jewish leaders wanted to silence him.

Paul returned to Jerusalem to plead his case and explain what he was doing and undoubtedly to preach Jesus to the Jewish leaders. Before he did anything, Jews from Greece and Asia Minor arrived and spread false stories about Paul. They stirred up a mob who grabbed Paul and wanted to kill him.

Just like Jesus, they handed Paul over to the Roman governor as the Jewish leaders tried to get someone to condemn him to death. The Roman governor could not find enough evidence to pronounce a guilty verdict. However, worried that the Jewish leaders would incite a riot, he did not release Paul, but kept him imprisoned in the city of Caesarea indefinitely.

Several years later, the next governor appointed to the region also failed to condemn him. But fearing the political power of the Jewish leaders, he was ready to send Paul back to them to stand trial.

Paul knew he would not survive back in Jerusalem. The leaders would find a way for him to have an "accident" that would claim his life. He played the only card he had remaining: he appealed his case to Caesar. As a Roman citizen, he had this right of appeal, and it required that he travel to Rome to present his case in person.

Paul's Fourth Missionary Journey to Rome

The Roman Governor assigned Paul a military guard and sent him by sea to Rome. The journey was long and arduous. Along the way, they sailed during winter storms and shipwrecked. All along, Paul remained confident that he would make it to Rome and served as an encouragement to the others, who despaired.

For several years, Paul remained in Rome, waiting for his day before Caesar. During this time, he wrote letters to the churches that comprise many of the epistles in our Bible.

The Jewish leaders failed to appear to present their case, and ultimately, the guards released Paul. But Acts ends with Paul preaching to all who would hear him in the capital. His story is evidence of the ever-expanding reach of the Church that Jesus promised to build. Paul encountered substantial opposition in his missionary work. However, the power of Jesus through the Holy Spirit was sufficient grace to see him through every trial.

The Acts of the Apostles show us the enormous impact that the life and death of Jesus had on people. Galilean fishermen became effective orators and preachers. Jewish persecutors became missionary apostles. The dynamite power of God through the Holy Spirit continued to break down barriers and produce the work of salvation in the lives of those who had heard.

The early church laid down a template for what "church" was supposed to be. The community of believers cared for one another and provided for each other when the times became difficult. We often look back at the "first-century church" through lenses that elevate their worship and community to an ideal that we desire to emulate.

The Apostle Paul laid the framework for thousands of missionaries to come. His willingness to go where people needed to hear about Jesus has inspired men and women to leave the comfort of home and set off in danger and trials to deliver the eternity-changing gospel of Jesus.

> "How beautiful are the feet of those who preach the good news!"
>
> Romans 10:15

Gospel Application

The life of Apostle Paul shows what a life of mission and service looks like. As a missionary, he had to tell others of the change that Jesus had made in his life. It didn't matter if the journey was easy or hard; he wanted to share the gospel.

Reading Paul's actions, we understand how the early church spread across the Roman Empire. He was tireless in his efforts to tell everyone he could.

Through Paul's travels and service, we gain clarity on the global and multi-cultural reach of the gospel. God's plan reached beyond any person or group. Everywhere Paul went, the gospel changed lives. It didn't matter if the person had any previous connection to God. The Holy Spirit brought faith and a new heart to anyone who believed in faith.

But Paul's travels also highlighted the opposition to the gospel. That opposition continues through this day. The methods may be different, but the resistance is there. Paul illustrated for us we do not have a straightforward path to walk as believers in Jesus.

The spread of the gospel also confirmed the centrality of the church the new Christian faith. Everywhere he went, the apostle planted churches. They served as the centers for worship, remembering Jesus, and support for one another. He appointed and qualified leaders to lead the church and train the people to know and follow the truth.

10

ERROR AND INSTRUCTION

ROMANS - JUDE

The book of Acts describes how the Apostle Paul planted churches on his missionary journeys. He wasn't the only one planting churches. Before long, there were churches all over the world. But since Christianity was so new, the early believers fell prey to false teaching and ignorance about the truth of the Gospel.

To combat this error, Paul and others wrote letters. They instructed people in the truth, refuted error, and praised them for remaining faithful. These letters form much of our New Testament. Out of the twenty-seven books, twenty-one are letters written to believers to address issues or errors that were growing in the church. They vary in length from the very hefty Romans and 1 Corinthians (16 chapters) down to the book of 2nd John (13 verses).

We find the letters after the book of Acts and before the book of Revelation. Together all they provide instruction on how to live the Christian life. Often, the new Christians fell for false teaching. Other times, they needed to be reminded of the truth they already knew.

Human authors wrote these letters, but the Holy Spirit inspired the writing. They were practical to meet the needs of the initial readers in whatever circumstance they found themselves. But they are the words of God for us today.

In his second letter to Timothy, the Apostle Paul describes the purpose and function of scripture.

> All Scripture is breathed out by God and profitable for **teaching**, for **reproof**, for **correction**, and **training** in righteousness, that the man (or woman) of God may be complete, equipped for every good work.
>
> 2 Timothy 3:15-16

In these two verses, Paul lays out a comprehensive system of maturation that is enabled and driven by the word of God.

1. Teaching. The meaning of this word is to instruct in the truth. God's word teaches us the truth about God and ourselves and how we ought to live.
2. Reproof. To reprove means to point out or identify errors. This means that when we stray from the truth, the Bible shows us the error of our ways.
3. Correction. This means that the Bible adjusts our lives to bring us back into line with the truth. This correction can be gentle or more direct, but the goal is to return us to living the right way.
4. Training. Just as we train to become proficient at physical activities, the Bible trains us in spiritual

matters. Through practice and repetition, we become better at living in the truth.

The people in the early church were all converts from some other religious system. They carried habits and preferences for how to worship God in their Christian faith. This led to conflict and problems.

In the early days of the church, unscrupulous people saw new believers as ripe for deception. These wolves in sheep's clothing came to the church and tried to take advantage of the believers. Passing themselves off as knowledgeable, they led the flock astray.

The early church needed clarity and instruction. These letters were God's answer to His people.

Fast forward two thousand years and the Church still struggles. Good Christians fall victim to false teachings and misapply the truth, twisting it in ways never intended. These letters to the early church are equally essential for us today.

The Bible is God's word. Every word. It's profitable for us to study it and apply it to our lives.

The Epistles Teach Sound Doctrine

We find sound doctrine taught throughout the letters of the New Testament. Doctrine is teaching that we affirm to be true. This means that the epistles teach the truth. It would be impossible to list all the sound doctrines that we find in these books. These few examples will illustrate the kinds of truth we find.

The Bible identifies humanity's natural standing before God. If you want a sobering read, look at the first three chapters of Paul's letter to the Romans (the Christian church that met in Rome). In painstaking detail, Paul builds a case that humanity is sinful and stands condemned before a holy God.

Romans 3:23 summarizes this simply when it says, "All have sinned and fall short of the glory of God." It is the cherry on the top of three hard-hitting chapters that don't pull any punches.

The reality of our sinful state leads us to cry out for a Savior. Trapped in the guilt of our sin, there is no other way that we can escape the deserved wrath of God. That was Paul's intention. He wanted his readers to be clear about where they stood, apart from the grace of God.

The letter to the church in Philippi explained how Jesus could be both God and man at the same time. In chapter two of his letter, Paul explained how Jesus set aside His divine rights without giving up His divinity so that He could become human and subject Himself to the humiliation of public execution.

This is a hard concept to comprehend. How can one person be two things at the same time? Paul offered an explanation that provides some information but does not answer every question. However, even though it doesn't have all the answers, Paul offered the assurance that Jesus came as both God and man. Because He was human, He could be a perfect representative sacrifice for us. But because He was God, he could satisfy the full demands of the Law.

Without this revelation, we might wonder about our salvation. Instead, it gives us information and insight that anchors us to the truth that was revealed to the Apostle Paul.

The Bible introduces us to spiritual gifts and explains that the Holy Spirit gives every believer spiritual gifts to contribute to their local body. The church in Corinth had misapplied this teaching and was making a mess of things. Paul wrote to them in 1 Corinthians 12 to set the record straight.

The Old Testament did not explain spiritual gifts in very much detail. There was little information for the early Christians to follow to understand this amazing thing that had happened to them. Fortunately, Paul's Holy Spirit-fueled letter provided just what they needed, and what we need, to understand what the Spirit does for us.

This teaching also instructs us in the truth that every believer has a role to play in the life of their church. There are no spectator gifts. Everyone has a contribution to make. Everyone takes part in the mission by serving one another.

The Epistles Tackle Error

Even though the early church had the Apostles, local churches still found their way into many false teachings. Today we are no better off. We are just as likely to stray from the truth of God's word and need to be shown the error of our ways.

In the very short book of Jude, the author wrote to a group of believers to point out to them the dangers of listening to false teachers who would lead them away from the truth into apostasy.

> For certain people have crept in unnoticed, who long ago were designated for this condemnation, ungodly people who pervert the grace of our God into sensuality and deny our only Master and Lord, Jesus Christ.
>
> Jude 1:5

Jude reminded his readers of what God had reserved for those to turn from the truth. He pointed to the fate of the Egyptians, the fallen angels, and even the residents of Sodom and Gomorrah. His warning was loud and clear about straying from the path into false teachings.

To the people in the churches of Galatia, Paul wrote of an encounter he had with the Apostle Peter. Peter had been living among Gentiles and had adopted some of their practices. But when he came to Jerusalem, he suddenly returned to the Jewish practices. This added fuel to the raging debate of whether the gentile Christians also had to become Jewish converts.

Paul confronted Peter about his hypocrisy and said that he was leading a poor example. The gospel liberated people–it did not bind them to old rules and requirements. The Jewish desire to force the gentiles into a Hebrew mold was misguided and needed to be stopped.

The error was the extra burden of following Jewish law. Christ had fulfilled the law and given us the gospel. It was wrong to return to the restrictions of that law, even though that way of life may have been comforting and familiar to some.

In his first letter to the church in Corinth, Paul spent most of chapter five chastising the church for allowing people who were living in unrepentant sin to continue in the church without rebuke or correction. Paul puts his finger right on the key aspect and tells them that this behavior was not God-honoring and they needed to address it right away.

The Epistles Offer Encouragement and Exhortation

The Epistles are not all bad news and correction. They also encourage us we have found something much better than we ever had before and that we are children of the King.

Hebrews chapter eleven, often called "Faith's Hall of Fame," celebrates the faith of many of the eminent men and women of the Old Testament. We have them as examples to show us what faith in action looks like. They filled the entire chapter with person after person and pointers to their great faith.

Since we have such a crowd of examples, we should to pursue faith on our own. We follow the same God as all these great people. And we have seen the mystery of the Gospel revealed in Jesus. The Old Testament saints were looking forward, placing their faith in God to provide a way. We know Who the way is, so what God has for us should bring us excitement.

First John chapter four is often called the love chapter because the Apostle John exhorts his readers to love one another.

> Beloved, let us love one another, for love is from God, and whoever loves has been born of God and knows God.
>
> 1 John 4:7

Because we know God and we have experienced His love, we are in a unique position to understand what love is really like. We have experienced it more deeply and broadly than mere human love. Therefore, we ought to reflect the love that we have received.

In his letter to the church in Ephesus, Paul described our fight against "the evil one." Paul used the metaphor of a soldier in full armor, deploying against the enemy. Paul helpfully gives us our orders: "Stand Firm!"

We do not need to defeat the devil. Jesus has already done that. We simply need to resist him by standing firm. And to do this, God has given us exactly the armor and tools we need to succeed.

Paul exhorts us to stand firm because Jesus has already won the battle. Because of this victory, we should find encouragement today. It should not intimidate us to see evil and wickedness in the world.

The Epistles Instruct in Church Practice

Since the church was a new institution and Jesus promised He would build the church, He also instructed those early congregations how to live as the church. In the epistles, we find practical instructions for how the church ought to function.

In Titus and 1 Timothy, Paul describes the criteria for people to become leaders of the church. Without these standards, the church risked falling for attention seekers and power mongers who wanted to use the status of the church for their purposes.

Paul provided very clear standards and qualifications for these leaders. It gave the churches the ability to discern between leaders and dangerous wolves in sheep's clothing.

In his letter to the Corinthians, Paul instructed how to conduct their church services. Their worship services had devolved into chaos. Gluttony and selfishness had infected the celebration of the Lord's Supper and people had created a value system of spiritual gifts that didn't align with God's purpose at all.

Paul wrote to them to rebuke them and provide clear teaching on the proper way to use gifts and take communion. He wanted them to straighten out their practices to bring glory to God. Since God has not changed, these instructions for how to worship God apply to us today.

Peter, himself a pastor, wrote about the proper function and role of a pastor in the church. It was not an exalted role, wielding power over the church. The pastor was to consider himself an under-shepherd. He did not have the authority of his own but received a commission from the over-shepherd, who is Jesus.

This was a foreign concept in the early church. But even today, we see people who try to grab any platform and use it for their ends. Fortunately, God has provided us with the instruction that we need to not fall into that trap and live lives that bring glory to Him.

These are only a few examples of what we find in the epistles. To learn more, it's great to dive in and study God's communication with us. There is much practical wisdom and effective correction and instruction in them.

The Epistles Are Not "Better"

Many people think the epistles are the best parts of the Bible because they address people like us today. They most directly address situations that are familiar and relevant to us today. These people create a hierarchy of books of the Bible and place the epistles at the top.

This is not accurate or appropriate. The entire Bible is God's inspired word. Every bit was "breathed out" by the Holy Spirit. We cannot say that any part of God's communication is better than any other part.

The epistles certainly have a direct application to us today. However, we cannot elevate them over other parts of the Bible lest we fall into error ourselves. We find amazing divine truth on every page and should not be partial.

Gospel Application

Even though the gospel had changed lives and exchanged hearts if stone for hearts of flesh, those people were still prone to error and being led astray. The Epistles provided clarity and instruction to resist false teaching. The Epistles explain the details and implications of the gospel so we can better understand how to follow Jesus.

Through the collection of letters in the Bible, we discover that the life of faith is more than just having faith. That faith must transform our lives to become more like Jesus. As the redeemed ones, we are called to live a life that shows the fruits of the Holy Spirit in our lives.

The Epistles offer tension between resisting error and pursuing right living. It isn't enough to just do one or the other. We are called to remain faithful to the gospel and to live lives that display its power.

11

AND THEN COMES THE END

REVELATION

We've now come to the end of the Bible. The book of Revelation serves as the matching bookend to the book of Genesis. But just because this is the last book, we're not done with the story of the Bible by a long shot. This last book packs a big punch!

The Apostle John wrote Revelation about forty years after Paul's epistles. He penned it while in exile on a small island in the Mediterranean Sea. It wasn't a book that he planned to write, but under the power of the Holy Spirit, he received a message through a series of visions, intended for the churches of his day.

In chapter one, John described how the book came about. While worshipping on a Sunday, he heard a voice and turned to see a vision of Jesus. John could make no mistake about who he saw. He spent three years with Jesus and became known as the disciple that Jesus loved. He even saw Jesus on the Mount of Transfiguration. When he saw the vision, he knew exactly who he was looking at.

In Revelation 1:19, Jesus instructed John to write about three different topics.

1. What John saw
2. Things that are
3. Things that will be

What John Saw

John saw a vision of the glorified Jesus. Standing amongst seven lamps, Jesus filled John's sight. John described Jesus as a human wearing a white robe with a golden sash. He had white hair and glowing eyes. His feet were dark but shiny and His voice washed over John in a rush of sound. In one hand he held seven stars and words came out of His mouth as sharp as a sword.

Jesus' face shone as bright as the sun. That wasn't a gentle glow. It was a radiant light that hurt John's eyes.

When John saw Jesus, the beloved disciple fell at His feet, unmoving. John knew he was unworthy to be in the presence of such glory and holiness. But Jesus raised John and began speaking to him.

Jesus explained the vision to John. He was standing in the middle of His church. The lamps represented seven churches, and the stars in His hand represented the messengers, or angels, of those churches. John was looking at Jesus, the head of the church, standing in power and glory amongst those whom He had called.

Jesus instructed John to capture the revelation and send it to seven churches around the Roman province of Asia Minor (modern-day Turkey). Jesus had a message for each of the churches, and He wanted John to write it down and send it to them.

The Things That Are

Jesus gave John specific messages to seven churches. These were not all the churches in existence. We saw many other churches that Paul planted in the book of Acts. However, the number seven represents perfection or completion, so in these seven churches, we find all the churches of John's day (and through to today) represented.

Serving as Jesus' scribe, John wrote the message that Jesus had for each of the seven local churches. Each of the churches had a distinct set of strengths and weaknesses. Some were doing well. Others were not on mission properly. Jesus called out what He saw in their corporate life and issued corrections and instructions for each church.

How would you respond if Jesus sent a personal letter to your church? What if you could read Jesus' assessment of the strengths and weaknesses, faithfulness, and disobedience of your church? Do you think you'd be happy? Or would you like to find a place to hide from His gaze?

Our churches today will not receive a dictated message from Jesus. But we can look at the seven messages that Jesus delivered and find our church represented in that list and hear His message for us.

The Message to Ephesus

Ephesus was a significant metropolis and the commercial center of the entire province of Asia Minor (modern-day Turkey). It had a large port on the Aegean Sea and was famous for its temple to Diana, which was listed as one of the seven wonders of the ancient world.

Paul founded the church and sent his protégé, Timothy, to be the pastor there. Paul visited at least twice and wrote three letters to Ephesus, one to the church and two to Timothy. John also spent many of his later years in Ephesus.

Jesus' message to the church in Ephesus was a commendation of how well they held to the true faith. But they had abandoned their first love. They followed the rules very well, but there was no heart or emotion in their worship. Jesus called upon this church to repent and return to how they were when they first believed in Him.

The Message to Smyrna

The city of Smyrna also had a port on the Aegean Sea and considered itself a rival of Ephesus. But the church's similarity with Ephesus ended there. Instead of being powerful, the community persecuted the church and the people who attended were poor, common people.

Jesus' words to the church in Smyrna were of compassion and praise. He knew they were facing persecution and even martyrdom for their faith. Yet they persevered, and the church continued to flourish and grow.

The Message to Pergamum

Pergamum was an ancient city of learning and a cultural seat. It also featured multiple temples to the Roman emperors and a strong pagan culture. Despite this ungodly culture, the church there persevered. Even though they experienced sharp persecution, their faith remained strong.

However, Jesus accused them of tolerating false teachers. Jesus named several false teachers or systems of heretical thought. While the leaders of the church didn't embrace these teachings themselves, they permitted teachers in their midst and did not take action to apply discipline or remove them from the body.

The Message to Thyatira

The city of Thyatira had very little to commend it. Many trading guilds operated out of the city. Perhaps because of the power of these guilds, the church made compromises in their teachings. Jesus acknowledged that their later activities were better than their former activities. They were growing in zeal for their faith.

But Jesus had no tolerance for their compromise. Even worse than the ideas of compromise, they tolerated a "Jezebel" in their midst. This leader claimed to be Christian, but actively lead the church into sexual sin, most likely in pagan rites in the local temples. Jesus promised a sound judgment upon this person and upon all who aligned themselves with her.

The Message to Sardis

Sardis was a ruined city. Beset by pride and false confidence, first the Persian and then the Romans had conquered the city. In AD 17, a tremendous earthquake devastated the city, and it never recovered. Now eighty years later, the church there resembled the city. Jesus had very little positive to say to the church. Beyond acknowledging a few individuals in the church who held to the true faith, His words were all judgment.

Jesus called the church at Sardis "dead." Even though they were active and appeared to be vital, He could see the truth of their hearts and they were lifeless. He told them that if they did not wake up, He would come as a thief and take away even what they had.

The church at Sardis stands as a warning for us today that just calling ourselves a church is not enough to please Jesus. He expects to see life and fruit coming from our service.

The Message to Philadelphia

The same earthquake which ruined Sardis also damaged Philadelphia. However, the city recovered and became a leading city in the center of the Anatolian peninsula. The church here was the only other message recipient who received no condemnation from Jesus. He recognized their perseverance, even though they had little power in this world.

Jesus promised to set straight the "synagogue of Satan" who afflicted the church in Philadelphia. This group of people, who must have advocated a form of Judaism as a prerequisite for Christianity, claimed to be loved by God more than the others. But Jesus promised to bring them low and show them He loved His church, and not them.

The Message to Laodicea

Laodicea was a wealthy city, with a prominent banking guild. The city also had earthquake problems, but was wealthy enough that it refused Rome's offer to help them rebuild. In this, they were proud and self-sufficient. The church there was neither on fire nor dead. Jesus had no praise for them. He knew their works, and they were "neither hot nor cold".

Because of their lukewarm faith, Jesus promised if they didn't change, He would spit them out of his mouth. Were they to be on fire, He would appreciate the passion of their zeal. Were they to turn away from Him entirely, He would bring correction to them according to their deeds. But they were apathetic, in the middle, and therefore of no use to Him.

The Lesson of the Churches

In Jesus' messages to these seven churches, we receive a clear insight into the heart of our Lord. He valued passionate service. Often, He commended churches for clinging to the truth in the face of persecution and opposition. Those churches that refused to turn aside from this faithful path received the best messages.

By the same token, He had harsh words for those churches which did not follow the gospel. The churches that allowed false teachers to take hold were offensive to Him. The

Ephesian church, who left the passion of their first love, received a similar judgment.

To the degree that our churches today have similar characteristics, we can identify the opinion that Jesus would hold of them. He is not grateful for any church that puts His name on the door. Even today, He seeks churches that are sold out to Him and fully in love with Him.

Revelation chapters two and three stand as a testimony to us today for how we should function as churches. We receive warnings of errors to avoid. We are told what our Savior desires of us. Our churches today would do well to take the admonition of these churches and apply them to our churches today as well.

The Things That Will Be

Following the messages to the churches, John received a vision of things that were going to happen. He saw these events as symbolic and apocalyptic images that he translated into words for us today.

In Matthew 24, near the end of His public ministry, Jesus' disciples asked Him when He planned to come in power. Jesus told His disciples that no one knew the day or the hour that He would come as the ruler. Only God in His omniscience knew that.

The Bible discusses the coming of God to reclaim the Earth and establish His rule. In the Old Testament, it's often called "The Day of the Lord." It's the coming of God to right all wrongs, establish justice on Earth, and punish those who have earned His wrath.

Revealing none of the timing, John observed what must come to pass for the Day of the Lord to arrive.

This part of the book of Revelation is hard to read and even more difficult to understand. It communicates through image and metaphor rather than clear language. But from it, we can draw some insights about the end of days and the coming new order.

Jesus Revealed as the Redeemer Lamb of God

John saw a new vision where he witnessed the worship of God on His throne. John carefully described a vision of the royalty and majesty of God. The description was almost poetic, suggesting that it was too wonderful for a clear description. John could only try to paint pictures with images and word pictures to give us a hint of what he saw.

Into this perfect worship scene, John discovered a problem. In His hand, God held a scroll, rolled tight, and sealed it to prevent it from being opened. Looking around the throne room, no one satisfied the requirements of opening the scroll. No angel or heavenly being, or even God Himself, could crack the seal and read the contents.

What was the scroll?

Based on the description of the scroll in Revelation 5:1, it appears to be a title or deed. The verse says that it had writing inside the scroll and on the outside of the scroll. We read of a similar scroll in the book of Jeremiah 32:6-12. Inside the scroll was the title for a piece of land. The outside described the terms of who could open the document or claim it.

Ever since Adam had declared his rebellion against God, Satan had been the ruler of the earth. When he tempted Jesus in Matthew chapter 4, Satan offered to trade rulership of the world to Jesus if only Jesus would worship him. Paul also called Satan the "prince of the powers of the air" in Ephesians chapter six.

Seeing this, John broke down and wept. He knew what the scroll contained. If nobody could redeem the scroll, then Satan and his evil ways would continue to reign on earth.

But then an unfamiliar figure stepped forward. John recognized Jesus, now appearing as a sacrificed lamb, as He came forward and claimed the scroll.

When Jesus arrived, all heaven broke out in song. Everyone in the throne room bowed down and praised the worthy name of Jesus. Thousands upon thousands of angels burst forth with one voice, singing of the greatness and glory of Jesus. He had become human, satisfied the law, and paid the price to meet the terms of the scroll. He could reclaim the title and bring about the Day of the Lord.

Jesus opened the scroll and unleashed judgment on Earth

As Jesus opened the seals on the scroll, God's judgment poured out upon the earth and the people who lived on it. God no longer held back. He unleashed the full measure of His judgment.

John saw this judgment but may not have understood everything he saw. He describes the judgments in apocalyptic and poetic terms that make it very hard to imagine how such things could happen.

God's wrath touched everything. The sun, the moon, and stars diminished by one-third. Earthquakes shook the ground. The oceans and rivers became poisonous and unfit for drinking or fishing. War and famine covered the earth and people died in multitudes. Demonic beasts roamed the earth, tormenting everyone they encountered.

John wrote of three rounds of seven judgments that God unleashed upon the earth. An action in heaven started each judgment (breaking a seal, blowing a trumpet, pouring out a bowl). He witnessed a fourth round, but when he wrote about it, an angel stopped him, saying it was too terrible to share.

Humanity responds to God's Judgment

While God's judgment rained down on the earth, John could see how people responded. A ruler of peace emerged to broker a treaty in the Middle East. After only three and a half years, however, he betrayed the treaty and instead of protecting Israel, he turned upon them.

With God's restraining presence removed, John saw Satan place two leaders over the earth to bring about his wicked scheme and attempt one more time to foil God's plans. These two leaders, one political and one religious, instituted a one-world government and religion. In very short order, they copied God's miracles to claim to be worthy of worship themselves.

As God's judgment rained down, people on the earth did not turn toward Him in repentance. Instead, they turned to Satan's puppets and declared their allegiance to the ruler of the Earth. The harder God's punishment affected them, the more they turned away from God.

Finally, in a last desperate move, John saw all the armies of the earth gathered in the Valley of Megiddo in Israel, to march on the last outpost of God's covenant people, Israel. These armies would accomplish Satan's objectives and prevent God from returning to fulfill His promises to His people. If they killed the people of God, then God could not keep his promise of an eternal covenant and an eternal kingdom.

Jesus Returns, Victorious

With the armies of the world gathered and on the brink of wiping out God's people, John saw Jesus return to Earth. John knew Jesus in the first coming. Jesus was meek and mild. This time, however, Jesus came in power and might, with an army of the redeemed at His back.

He did not need the army. Jesus simply spoke a word, and John saw the armies defeated in a single stroke. The devastation of the battle of Armageddon represented a decisive victory for Jesus over Satan's power.

This was the Revelation from which the book derived its name: Jesus revealed as the Lord of all. None could stand against Him.

Revelation 20 described what John saw after Christ's return. Jesus sat on the throne and ruled over the Earth for a thousand years. No one could deny His absolute authority. Of Satan's rule, nothing remained, for Satan himself was bound away and not allowed access to the Earth.

At the end of this time, John saw Satan released from his restrictions one last time and returned to his pattern of opposing God. Despite the ideal conditions on Earth, he found a group of followers and led a short-lived rebellion. But Jesus demolished the uprising and brought His final judgment upon Satan.

Jesus as the Judge

John saw Jesus sitting on a throne of power, judging the people of the earth who were finally called to account for their deeds. It did not matter how they fared in their life. Every living person came forth and faced the judgment of God.

In this judgment, there were only two outcomes. God accepted with names written in the Lamb's Book of Life. Covered by the blood of Jesus, they did not suffer judgment, but He welcomed them as sons and daughters.

The Righteous Judge found everyone else guilty and sentenced them to punishment. As a holy God, He could not overlook sin. Every sin demanded punishment, and He could no more turn away from that punishment than He could sin Himself.

This scene is called "The Great White Throne Judgment". It was the final judicial act of God over His creation. At the end of the judgment, the slate was clean, all sin had been paid for. Some He had invited into His household. Others He condemned to the lake of fire and brimstone for an eternity separated from God.

A New Heaven and Earth

John finally witnessed the destruction of the Earth and the heavens above it. Tarnished by sin, they needed to be wiped clean. In a new act of creation that mirrored Genesis 1, John saw God create a new Heaven and a New Earth. In this sin-free place, God's glory was on display for all to see.

People lived on the earth and rather than a new sun to provide their light, the glory of God lighted their days. His light shone through the walls of the city of the New Jerusalem, which seemed to orbit the New Earth, bringing day and night with every rotation.

Gospel Application

Revelation brings us full circle from the book of Genesis. Here we see the culmination of God's redemption and the promises He made to His people. We see how His plan came about just as He planned, even though from our human perspective, events around us might seem to be out of control and heading in the wrong direction.

In the book of Revelation, we learn how God planned to bring about justice and judgment, in His own time and way. We see it figuratively so that we cannot directly map our current events into a specific timeline that tells us when these things are going to happen.

But most of all, we see the glory of God on display. He will not stand by and turn a blind eye to sin. He has kept records of what has been done and will ensure that every act is called into account. But the blood of Christ covers sins so that those who received forgiveness did not go through this judgment. He received them into His family as sons and daughters.

Revelation ends on an optimistic, glorious note. God will dwell amongst His creation and the forgiven will dwell with Him forever. And so shall we ever be with the Lord.

PUTTING IT ALL TOGETHER

Since God is the author of the Bible, He tells the story we need to know. It's a story designed to draw us back to Him. Beginning with the estrangement in Genesis chapter two, He slowly reveals the plan which He had developed before He created the first atom of this world.

At all times, God was in control of this plan. It wasn't ever in danger of not coming to pass. Even though from a human perspective, things seemed out of control, God wasn't anywhere near a panic. Rather, He used every development to further the cause of what He wanted to come about.

Reading the Bible is an opportunity for us to see God in action. His actions reveal His character. We don't have to look at what He said, we can observe what He did. This is a much clearer picture of who He is and what He's about. Throughout the Bible, several characteristics jump off the page.

God's Patience

Not because the plan took a long time to unfold, but because He put up with disobedient, rebellious behavior from His people without losing His composure. Despite Israel's idolatry and fickleness, He did not change His mind or alter His plan.

God's Holiness

This is a fancy theological way of saying how much He hates sin. From the very beginning, we get to witness how destructive it is. One transgression had the impact of altering the relationship between all of humanity and our Creator. God consistently declares His holy standard and the terrible consequences for failing to meet it. Not because He wants to punish us, but because He won't let sin infect who He is. It's the ultimate zero-tolerance policy.

God's Love

When it came time to pay the penalty for sin, He did not pass the buck to some poor unwitting soul. He sent His Son. God Himself. He paid the price that we incurred. Only He could do it. And He knew that from the beginning. He created everything, knowing He would have to redeem it back at a tremendous cost.

This is what we should pick up from reading the Bible. These are the great truths about God that ground us and give us hope that all the promises will still come true. We haven't experienced freedom from the presence of sin. We haven't weathered the judgment for the penalty of sin.

We look forward with faith. Our hope is based on the character of the One who made the promises. Since He has proven to be trustworthy and reliable throughout the Bible, we have the hope that He will keep His promises to us.

Great Takeaways from the Bible

The story of the Bible hangs together despite the unlikely number of human authors and the extremely long period it took to write. It's not a human document, and it wasn't up to the individual authors to figure out what to say.

God superintended the entire book. That's the only explanation that makes any sense. Only if God managed the process could the story of the Bible hang together so well.

As we read the Bible, we see several themes come together clearly.

The Problem of Sin

No matter how we look at the Bible, sin must remain at the top of our awareness. It was the initial conflict that took nearly the entire book to find a resolution. And even then, it cost the life of the Son of God.

Sin shattered the relationship that Adam and Eve had with God. It is a lie to sugarcoat our sin. There is no way that we can call a sin "ok" or "small" when we see that something as seemingly trivial as taking a bite from a fruit created the entire human condition.

Minor sins are only small in our own eyes. God, who sees everything perfectly, clearly knows that our sins drive a wedge between Him and us. He knows how devious and destructive sin can be. We want to excuse or justify our behavior.

One "small" sin created a problem that took over the story of the relationship between God and His creation. Calling it "nothing" denies the entire consequence of the story that the Bible is trying to work out for us.

We would do well from reading our Bible to see sin the same way that God does. All of it is deadly serious. And for those who have received forgiveness, we need to remember Whose blood spilled so that we could receive forgiveness from our sins.

The Failure of Human Effort

Even though God set up the institutions of governance and leadership, none of these institutions offered a long-term solution to our problem. Each of them provided only short-term, temporary relief from the consequences of our rebellion against God.

When God chose a leader to lead on His behalf, the only reason that the leader saw results was because God was working through them. The leader brought nothing meaningful to the situation.

It does not matter if we refer to a judge, a prophet, a priest, or a king. None of them provided a solution for the real problem that plagued humanity. Judges died, prophets had ungodly children, priests could only temporarily cover sin, and kings often led the people astray.

No matter how tempting it might be to think the spiritual grass is greener on the other side of some institutional fence, the Bible points out that the end of this thinking is always a failure. It's no different today because people haven't changed. As a race, we're still tainted by sin. Even though some have experienced the redemption of the cross, we cannot lead our way out of the predicament in which we find ourselves.

The Importance of Faith

If we cannot take any direct action to improve our spiritual condition before God, we must have faith that He will do something for us. Much of the Bible, the Old Testament, tells the story of people who never saw the payment for their sins. They died before Jesus was born.

But even though they lived before Jesus, their faith in God was what pleased Him. Because of this faith, He credited righteousness into their account. When Jesus died on the cross, His blood paid the price of the sins of those who looked forward to Him.

For us who live after the cross, we also must come to God by faith. Even though we understand the story and see the redemption at Calvary, we must have faith we cannot save ourselves and God, through Jesus can.

We live by faith even today. Our faith covers our present salvation and our future deliverance. When the Great White Throne Judgment occurs, we have faith that the blood of Jesus will cover our sins and God will accept us as sons and daughters rather than condemn us to punishment for eternity.

Salvation isn't something we earn. We must receive it as a gift. Only then can our sins be blotted out.

The Sovereignty of God

While it might be nice to dictate the terms of redemption or the timeline of the end, God is sovereign. He has His plan and only He knows it. He will bring about events in His good time.

As much as we think we understand a system of thought, we would do well to listen to Job after God showed up in his debate with the bad-advice-friends. God is so far above us we cannot step into His seat and determine what should happen, or who should suffer.

Our role is to recognize our dependence upon God and live in submission to His will. Only then will we align with the greatest power in the universe.

It might seem logical to us that something should happen soon. But God has His reasons for His timing, and we cannot understand why He chooses the events and timing that He does. We need to call Him God and remember that He created us. Only then can we find the correct perspective to understand our role in His creation.

The Simplicity of the Gospel

Even though Adam's rebellion created a complicated problem, God chose a simple resolution. He didn't require that we all become advanced theologians to understand the plan of salvation. It's so simple a small child could understand.

This is a major miracle of its own. Our sin problem is so pervasive and complicated, it touches everything we do. Yet God architected such a simple solution, we don't have to be educated to understand it or believe in it.

This is one of the greatest reasons we know God wrote the Bible to us. What matters is easily understandable. We don't have to study for years just to hope to comprehend the message of the Bible.

Adam disobeyed God, and the consequence of his decision was sin and death for all who followed.

Jesus completely obeyed God and gave the benefits of His righteousness to us, while accepting the punishment for our sins.

Open your Bible and dive in. Everything that matters is there for you to find. Along the way, enjoy the stories. But notice how they point to the need for a Savior or how they reveal the Savior. That's the simplicity of the Bible.

The important thing is that you listen to what God has to say.

TAKE THE NEXT STEP

Learning about the Bible as a whole is a great first step. But what comes next? Take the step to learn how to study God's Word in a book that explains the process in easy to understand language.

Study the Bible - Six Easy Steps

You'll find a proven study method that works for Bible students of all experience levels, explained in the same easy-to-read style. And as a bonus, you'll get a guided tour of your first Bible study.

For an up-to-date list of all my books and resources, visit my official website:

https://Dennis-Stevenson.com

ABOUT THE AUTHOR

I write books for everyday Christians who want to build their faith. I believe that you can have a rich and rewarding spiritual life - even if you didn't go to seminary, or learn how to read Greek and Hebrew. The tools of the Christian faith don't have to be a mystery. That's where I want to help.

I cut through the confusing terms and present spiritual truth in everyday language. I'll show you how to get the most out of your Christian life with the tools and knowledge you already have. I'll break it down until it makes sense and you can do it for yourself.

I grew up in a pastor's home. Some nights, the dinner table felt like a seminary classroom. But the result was that I was given a deep love of God and the Bible from a very early age. As an adult, I built on that foundation by pursuing learning and study on my own. I still haven't gone to seminary. I don't think that's necessary to pursue God. I have impressed God's word on my heart and made it central in my life.

I've been studying the Bible myself for over 30 years. For more than 20 of those years I've been teaching others what I know. This experience, both of study and teaching, has shown me what everyday Christians want to know, and how they like to learn it. As an author, my purpose is to capture what I know and give it to you

I'd love to connect with you! You can join the new releases list on my website at www.dennis-stevenson.com/stay-in-touch to learn about more books as they are published. This is the best way! You can also follow me online on my author page on Facebook at AuthorDennisStevenson.

Printed in Great Britain
by Amazon

84488117R00098